TIFFANY REED BRILEY

FILLED

HIS PRESENCE, OUR PURPOSE

LESSONS FROM A WELL

Published by Epiphany Publishing

© 2023 Tiffany Reed Briley

No part of this book may be reproduced or transmitted in any form or by any means, electronic or mechanical, including photocopying and recording, or by any information storage or retrieval system, except as may be expressly permitted in writing by the publisher. Requests for permission should be addressed in writing to the publisher.

Layout design and front cover image by Tiffany Reed Briley

Unless otherwise noted, all Scripture quotations are taken from the English Standard Version (ESV).

To order additional copies of this resource, order online or by email at tiffanyreedphotography@gmail.com.

DEDICATION

To my mother, Marlene, whose prayers altered the course of my life.

To my dad Bob Reed, who

welcomed his prodigal daughter home with open arms.

For my husband, the prince who finally appeared.

Acknowledgments

Sandy Spurrier and Stacy Reese, two of the most important people of my life. Long talks on the couch, tears, and laughter were the sacred moments that helped me become who I am. I'll never be able to thank my aunt enough for praying, for being relentless, and loving me as her own.

Darlene Platt, who forgave with profound amounts of grace. You showed me a side of Jesus that I hadn't known and I'll forever have a heart that is engraved with your name on it.

Missy Platt, whose tenderness and compassion had open arms waiting for me when I came home and perhaps became one of the most precious friendships of my life.

Lisa Anderson Barlean, my spiritual mentor, dearest friend, and kindred spirit. You held my hand as I asked hard questions. You lovingly inspired me to seek more intimacy with the Lord by observing your love relationship with Him. You speak into my life with so much wisdom and gentle guidance.

Katie Lee DePoppe, with every early morning cup of coffee you called me into creativity and stirred my soul with your contemplative conversations that called deep unto deep. You sharpen me, dearest. Your encouragement helped me believe that I could be a writer.

Rachelle Rea Cobb, without you telling me to stop researching and start writing, this birthing process may have never begun. Your encouragement is uplifting, inspiring and deeply appreciated. Your fingerprints on my work are precious to me.

To the women at The Gathering in Goose Creek who believed in this study and desired to journey through it with me.

To Stephanie Jones for pastoring me, helping me find healing and for providing a home for my weary heart at New Day. The time you invested in me and this new season is where I felt the Lord move me forward to publish this study.

And most importantly to the Lord who lifted my feet out of religion and invited me into an experiential relationship. You gave words to my heart and wrote the theme of this study. You are raw. You are beauty. You are filling. You are everything. I'm changed because of Your words in this study and honored that you entrusted me with these pages.

Table of Contents

PREFACE 11
Introduction: Two women, two stories 13
Week One: The Wishing Well 16
   Day One: A Place Of Beginnings 17
   Day Two: Significance Of The Well 24
   Day Three: Digging Our Well 30
   Day Four: Digging Deeper 36
   Day Five: Defining Our Purpose 41
Week 2 - Stories From The Well 47
   Day One: Isaac & Rebekah, Radical Faith Part 1 48
   Day Two: Part 2 - Isaac & Rebekah: Faith That Doesn't Wait 53
   Day Three: Jacob & Rachel: The Not So Perfect Fairy Tale 58
   Day Four: Hagar, The Story Of The Broken Part 1 66
   Day 5: Hagar, The Story Of The Broken Part 2 75
Week 3 – A Woman At The Well 81
   Day One: Broken, Is Her Name. 82
   Day Two: Expectations 86
   Day Three: Quenching Thirst 92
   Day Four: Leaving It Behind 96
   Day Five: Transformed, Unafraid, Unashamed 101
Week 4 - Refreshing Of The Lord 106
   Day One: Breaking Through And Beyond Barriers 107
   Day Two: His Refreshing 111
   Day Three: The Divine Pursuit 117
   Day Four: Worship In Spirit and Truth 124
   Day Five: Refreshed 129
Week 5 – Finding Our Well 134
   Day One: A Purpose Revealed 135
   Day Two: Divine Intimacy 142
   Day Three: Leaving Our Jar 150
   Day Four: Our Ministry 156
   Day Five: Jesus: Our Prince, Our First And Our Last 161
About The Author 166

PREFACE

I wasn't looking for a Bible Study to write. The book you are holding in your hands pummeled me in the most powerful and intensely personal way. It had all the markings of the Holy Spirit's fingerprints.

While studying the early church in Acts I moved to the book of John to look at Jesus's ministry with fresh eyes. There tucked in chapter 4 I found her. I had visited her before, but the Holy Spirit was pouring out newness on that chapter the woman recorded turned and looked me square in the eyes and I saw myself.

This study is intensely personal. The Lord engraved it on my heart. One week into research stopped me dead in my tracks with these words "I gave this to you, because you are the woman at the well". Even as I write those words tears well up in my eyes.

Through this lesson Jesus has been teaching me what it truly means to be a Woman of the Well, because that's where He found me. Right next to the well, broken.

Here at the well we'll grip our broken pieces together. It's my prayer your heart will be found mirrored in the pages, and that you'll meet Jesus in a fresh new way as your husband. It's only with Jesus that we can truly experience the intimacy we long for.

You see John chapter 4 and the woman at the well is not about a seedy whore, this account is about unmet longings and a heart that is searching. Oh how she was searching. This story is an echo of your own heart.

Together let's reach for our broken pieces and bring them to Jesus.

Tiffany

Introduction: Two women, two stories

Darkness slipped away as a sliver of sunrise seeped into the room through the small window. Light kissed her cheek while her eyes remained closed. Deep slow breaths began to speed up as her awareness began to calculate the day's responsibilities waiting for her. Weary she pushed herself off the bed and reached for her wrap to ward off the chill.

"Another day" she whispered to the empty room with a sigh.

When had life become so difficult? Gone were the childhood days of adventures and big dreams. When had they slipped away? Mundane repetition allowed her to move absently through her morning while completing what was required of her.

The sun rose higher and the earth with its occupants began their day. Opening the wooden door she heard the soft laughter of younger girls playing at their mother's feet while she worked.

It hadn't been so long ago that she twirled in a meadow with the warm sun dancing across her face as she spun with her sister. They passed the summer days as young ones dreaming dreams and telling each other tales of a prince who would one day come. It was a story passed down for generations.

Breathing deeply the morning air, she let her memories slip back to the stories of her childhood and she allowed herself just a moment to remember the dreams that had long since left her.

~

In a different time and different place a young woman stepped into the soft early morning light with a smile on her face. It was a new day. Fresh and alive with endless possibilities. A smile crept to her face as she whispered "Today. Maybe today".

"All it takes is one day to change your whole life" were the words her grandmother had repeated to her more times than she could count. "You just never know, dearest. So always be ready. A ribbon in your hair and a smile on your face". Now nearly a grown woman, she reached for her blue ribbon with a smile.

Reaching for her jar, she slipped out of the house and headed to the well-worn path. Mornings were her favorite. She adored the quiet and stillness before creation awoke. The sounds of nature surrounded her. Breathing deeply she lingered over a new bloom and gazed at the bird building her nest.

She reached the place she knew so well, and was thankful that she'd made the extra effort to arrive earlier than later. The moments of lost sleep were worth it when she could come to this place and enjoy the solitude before the morning rush began. Kneeling next to the stone she lifted her head as the sun began to peak over the mountain. Closing her eyes, she let the warmth seep into her soul.

This place was as familiar to her as an old friend. It was as if the well held more than water but also her secrets. Her wishes were poured out as she pulled the water in. The dreams of her heart whispered of a handsome prince that would make her his bride. It was all she wanted, all she dreamed of, and her purpose.

"One day" she whispered and with a deep breath and another wish in her heart, she lowered the pail to draw out the water. "One day, he'll come and find me. Let it be soon. A ribbon and a smile".

~

The story of a young maiden longing for her prince is as familiar to little girls as their own name. It's a story rooted deeply within us with its seeds sown carefully into our hearts.

Our homes may look very different, our customs may be wide spread, but the one thing that ties all of our hearts in unity is the dream that emerges from our childlike hearts. It's the song from the wishing well. It's the hope of the girl who after being misunderstood, ignored, or overlooked who comes to the well and is found. Waiting for her is Prince with a smirk on His face and adventure in His eyes.

This very desire that etches itself into our young hearts was placed there for a purpose and it might be quite different from what you think. Let's jump into the study of the Wishing Well, and maybe just maybe we'll not only find our Prince, but we might also find our purpose.

Week 1: The Wishing Well

Day One: A Place Of Beginnings

"Then the Lord appeared to Abram and said "To your offspring I will give this land. So he built an altar to the Lord, who had appeared to him."

Genesis 12:6

Bible Reading: Genesis 12: 1 - 9

PRAY ALOUD AND ASK THE LORD TO OPEN YOUR EYES TO THE TRUTH HE HAS WAITING FOR YOU, AND ASK HIM TO TUNE YOUR EARS TO HEAR HIS VOICE.

A story without a setting are only words. Today we'll begin journey to the well by entering the historic town of Shechem. So pack your bags, grab your sunglasses, and lets step back into the historic Holy Land.

If you've traveled to the Holy Land, you'll know much of it is a desert. Tucked away like an oasis is a historic town that you can visit today. If you were to travel there you'd be looking for a town called Nablus, but we'll call it by its historic name, Shechem. Located between two mountains (Ebal & Gerizim), this small town is just 34 miles north of Jerusalem. Streams from the springs flow down the slopes of the valley causing it to be a place of abundance for crops, vegetation and life.

Shechem will become familiar to you as you return regularly over the coming weeks. By the time we close on this study, we'll have crossed from the start of the Old Testament all the way to Jesus and back again while remaining in this very town. The significance of this place will be a fundamental piece of our time together and I hope it becomes dear to your heart. Before we begin, let's set the stage for our exploration.

We will pick up our journey under an ancient oak tree where we find the Lord appearing to Abram.

Open your Bible Genesis 12:1.

What was the first word that the Lord gave to Abram as recorded in Scripture?

_____

Now let's travel to the New Testament and thumb over to the book of James chapter 2, verse 23.

Who did what: _____

He was called: _____

Our study starts with obedience and we will find that this theme runs throughout our time together. In the book of James we see that Abraham believed God and because of that he was called God's friend.

> *Because Abraham believed what God told him, relationship was established.*

REFLECTION:

What is one trademark of your closest relationship?

If you mentioned that honesty, communication or trust was a vital factor to your closest relationship, it might surprise you that God feels exactly the same way.

Back in Genesis 12:1, the Lord said to Abraham "go". In verse 4, we see that Abraham "went". What it doesn't say is "Abraham pondered this decision". Or Abraham "pulled out his life planner and started strategizing". Nope, he just packed his bags and went.

REFLECTION:

As you reflect, can you recall the last thing the Lord asked you to do?

If you struggle to answer this question, don't worry. Before we finish today we're going to jump into a few tips that I use in my personal quiet time with the Lord that help me hear His voice a little more clearly.

We are years away from the garden of Eden, the flood and the days of Noah have long since passed. The tower of Babel was built and the Lord has scattered the people across the earth. Here we find in Genesis 12 that God calls a man named Abram to stand out from his generation.

As previously mentioned, one important key to note is that God doesn't direct him where to go.

Let's just get real honest here. I'm not a Bible teacher that's going to be "preachy". I do real. I hope you will too. Now if God came to me and said "Go. Leave your country, your family, your folks, and go to a land I'll show you". I'd be looking at Him and saying "and where is that exactly?"

Wouldn't you? You know, I love the sisterhood. I do. We are intricate, creative, emotional wonders, but one of the challenges most of us have is that we are control freaks. Don't you agree? We love us some blueprints.

Put yourself in Abrams shoes for a moment. If tomorrow God tells you to leave everything and everyone and doesn't give an exact location, would you go? The stumbling block here isn't the calling, it's the trusting.

Look at verse 2. What are the 4 things God promises to Abram?

1.

2.

3.

4.

Remember these promises. This is going to be important. In fact, if you mark in your Bible, I want you to put a little #1 directly next to verse 2. Here we find the very first time the Lord makes a promise to Abram.

GOD MARK: During this study, we're going to unearth insights into the personality of the Lord. Look for GOD MARK and underline it in red when we come across these moments. Verse 6 is important because we find our first GOD MARK:

God delights in His children trusting Him and it's a precursor to His promises.

Notice that although God didn't tell Abram *where*, He *asked* him to take action and go. Once we do our part in that first step of obedience, God often times reveals the details.

Once Abram arrives at Shechem to the oak of Moreh, the Lord meets him there and makes him a promise. When Abram looks down at his feet, all that land surrounding him is going to be gifted by God to his children, grandchildren and all future generations. The life in this new land is promised to be bountiful and fruitful, but there's one small problem.

Jump over to Genesis chapter 11, verse 29 - 30.

Who was Abram's wife _____

What defined her: _____

Problem! His wife isn't able to have children. I'm so thankful that we serve a God who does the impossible. I can imagine God smiling at this couple saying, "You're barren? No problem. I've got this, and a small detail like barrenness won't hold back my plans".

Moment of candor:

Girls, let me be vulnerable with you. I'm speaking to you from a place of barrenness. As I write this study, I've been married for ten years and there's no sign of a baby anywhere in sight. To make matters more interesting, I feel that for the last 14 years that God has been preparing my heart that I won't be a mother biologically.

I want to speak directly to those of you who are doing this study who are barren and have the longing for a child. This study is about bringing our brokenness, our longings, our mess (our hot mess), and our vulnerability to the well. We'll get into this more later, but I want you to know and hold this promise:

God's plan is that we be fruitful, multiple, fill the earth, be disciples that share the Gospel. One of the greatest callings on a woman's life is to be a wife and mother.

If you're at a place where your barrenness is a part of your brokenness, I want you to hold to the truth that I cling to:

> GOD WOULD ONLY WITHHOLD THAT MUCH JOY IF THERE WAS SOMETHING FAR GREATER AHEAD FOR YOU, OR MAYBE JUST MAYBE YOUR TIME HAS NOT YET COME.

For all of you who don't struggle with being barren, but do have a hole in your life this is for you as well. I want you to think about the one thing in your life that you feel is the hole to your joy. Is it finding a husband? Your dream job? The loss of your spouse or child? A loss of purpose, finances or sickness? It could be a broken home, broken dreams, or a broken child.

Write your longing below - because we'll identify this as our place of barrenness:

Let's jump back to Abram and look at what he did after He received this word from the Lord. First though, let's place a #2 next to verse 7. This is the second time we've seen a word from the Lord to Abram. It's a promise that seems like it's the impossible.

What was Abram's response?

Here we find Abram building an altar for the Lord. Why? Because God appeared to him in that place. This is important because by building the altar, he was marking, claiming and holding God to the promise. He was creating a physical marker to mark the unphysical.

Rather than picking up at the well, we're starting our journey intentionally with Abraham. It's important to note his obedience to the Words of the Lord because that obedience will set the pace and act as a starting point for our journey.

Abraham heard the word of the Lord and he immediately acted in obedience. It's interesting to note that the next time he would receive a Word from the Lord would be after he had acted in faith to 'go'. It wasn't just any word from the Lord that came out of Abram's initial obedience. He received a prophetic word and promise from the Holy One. To mark this occasion, he physically built an altar. Let's consider this a pillar that was constructed between him and God as a reminder of the Word.

There's no doubt that the physical action which marked the Word of the Lord set certainty in his heart brick by brick. Don't you think that each time Abraham walked by that altar on a daily basis that he was reminded of the promise and the Word of the Lord?

MAKING IT REAL:

Every now and then we'll come across a project. You can get as creative as you like. I want to encourage you to take the time to pour yourself into this.

Here is your first assignment:

Go find a ball jar, a clay jar, or a paper jar. Whatever you've got that will hold something, go rummage through your attic and grab it. Got it?

>Really - don't skip this. It will be important.

I want you to rewrite out your barrenness and place it in this jar. All the hurts, all the longings of your heart should go in this jar. If you're meeting as a group for this study, bring your jars to the next week's gathering and show them to each other. This is going to become a pivotal point in our study, so I want to encourage you to follow through.

TAKE ACTION:

If you feel deep in your heart that you were created for so much more than what life looks like right now, I want to strongly encourage you to read the following very carefully.

One of the game changers in my relationship with the Lord was when I started being intentional about being in a position where I can clearly hear the voice of the Lord. My prayer for the last 10 years has been that I would recognize His voice with the familiarity that I have when my husband calls my name. That being said, clearly hearing isn't enough. We're told to be 'doers of the word, and not hearers only'. Can you imagine what we might accomplish for the Lord if we acted on each Word that we were given? If we are trusted with the small words that were entrusted to us, we will be found faithful for the larger assignments.

Two years ago I started a practice in my quiet time that placed emphasis on the Words of the

Lord. Whenever I feel the Lord whisper something to my heart, or if it jumps off the page at me, I'll record the Word in red ink. Much like the words of Jesus recorded in the Bible, His words to me are recorded in red. Not only do I stop, switch pens, and make an intentional note of that which has been given to me, but it's also setting an altar in my journal. Several times a year, and even once a month I'll go back and look at the last Word from the Lord I've been given, and it's easy to find because it will be in red.

Have you ever felt like you were in a faith desert? It's a place where mind knows He's near, but your heart and soul feel like He's miles away dealing with other people and their issues. During this place of quiet I always draw back to my last Word received. When you are in a period of questioning the direction and presence of the Lord, go back to your last Word from Him and ask yourself the following question. "Did I do what he told me to do".

While you are working through this study, I want to encourage you to write in your book with a red pen. Record in that red ink the words or promptings you feel the Lord saying. If something on the page speaks to your heart, underline it in red. If God whispers something, jot it down in the margin in red.

At the end of each week, I want you to go back and review the words with red ink. Make a date with yourself and God at your favorite coffee shop, and soak in the precious Words that the Lord spoke over you.

Obedience to His voice through this study is vital. Hence the reason we're spending so much time with Abraham, his promise, his altar, and in the city of Schechem.

So girls, as we wrap up day 1, week 1, I hope you have your jar, your red pen and your journal ready for our trip. I'm so anxious for how the Lord is going to reveal Himself, His plans, His direction, and the tender Whispers waiting for us.

Day Two: Significance Of The Well

"He looked, and saw a well in the field, and behold, three flocks of sheep were lying there beside it, for from that well they watered the flocks. Now the stone on the mouth of the well was large. When all the flocks were gathered there, they would then roll the stone from the mouth of the well and water the sheep, and put the stone back in its place on the mouth of the well"

Genesis 29:2

PRAY ALOUD AND ASK THE LORD TO OPEN YOUR EYES TO THE TRUTH HE HAS WAITING FOR YOU, AND ASK HIM TO TUNE YOUR EARS TO HEAR HIS VOICE.

Bible Reading: Genesis 29:1-12

It's the story of the unrecognized, obscure, neglected girl, the persecuted heroine that we all know so well. The story first appears in antiquities that dates back 7 BC and the story of Rhodopis, a Greek slave girl who marries the king of Egypt. She is our earliest known "Cinderella".

Many of these fairy tales take place around wishing wells and regardless of whether the well is a prominent element of the story or briefly mentioned in passing, wishing wells are as familiar to us as the pennies we toss into them.

Originating out of European folklore, many consider the significance of wells coming from the deities that would dwell in the waters. They believed that the water would have been sacred and a source of life. They are correct, to an extent. But to gather the full story, we must go back to 'Once Upon A *Real* Time', to a land very different from Europe and further beyond. To immerse ourselves in the full story, we need to pick up our Bibles to find the truth in the wishing well.

As we study, we'll find that wishing wells are not merely fanciful notions created from the mind of Disney or the Brothers Grimm. In fact, I would suggest to you that these men were merely copying their secular version of the story from our master Creator who had set this plot in our heart from the time earth began, and that my dear friends is a tale worth being told.

The first mention of a well in Scripture is Genesis 16:14, but before we jump into that treasure that's waiting for us, let's gain a full and deeper knowledge about the significance of wells in the Bible.

We know due to the terrain of the middle east that sources of water would be vital to sustain life. While there are lakes and rivers in the middle east that would flow from the surface, a well that was dug deep into the earth could be protected from contamination if built properly and maintained.

Wells Acted As Territorial Boundaries

Whether it's Indiana Jones searching for the Holy Grail (the mythical cup of Christ that provided eternal life), or another storyline there have always been wars or conflict over life giving sources. Our ancient middle east wells are no different. Established as boundaries and claimed as territories it's no wonder that this life giving source would be staked and claimed.

Hand Dug And Built

Let's step out of our Starbucks, fast food, fast cars, fast paced lifestyle and strap on our robes, sandals and head coverings (because we would all be wearing them). Remember there were no drilling rigs that would aid these hard working men from locating and digging down deep to provide for their families. The labor required to hand dig a well in the blazing middle eastern sun would be a task to be sure. Without water their family, crops and livestock would never survive. It was a necessary and vital task. Whether or not your efforts produced water, was another story. An effort to localize a place to dig, and tap into a life giving source was critical.

They Required Supporting Walls

I can imagine that after hours of digging in sweltering heat, the site of water bubbling up from the ground would be cause for celebration. Once water was found, it would be important to fortify the hole with supporting walls to keep the area open for future collection of the water.

They Were Sealed To Prevent The Water Draining

Ancient middle east tradition tells us that once the walls were built, lime would be rubbed over the surface to ensure that as the water sprang up and was gathered it would be contained and not seep out.

They Were Protected

For those who had the ability to locate a water source below the ground, the manpower to dig and build the well, it would be vital to keep it from being overused or claimed by an enemy. The further away the well was from the settlement, the more protection would be required. Although this life source would be visited frequently by the shepherds of the settlement and the women of the village, it would be imperative to keep watch over it against enemy attack.

Let's look at our verse again for today and fill in the blanks. Open up to Genesis 29:2-3.

"He looked, and saw a _____, and behold, three flocks of sheep were lying there beside it, for from that well they watered the flocks. Now the _____ on the mouth of the well was _____. When all the flocks were gathered there, _____ would then roll the stone from the mouth of the well and water the sheep, and put the stone back in its place on the mouth of the well"

Not only would the mouth of the well need to be protected from enemies but it was also vital to have the well protected from contamination (natural or unnatural). For this reason and in our verse today we see that a large rock would have been kept over the opening of the well. To move that large rock many men would have gathered together to roll it away.

There Were Emotional Ties To The Well

Flash forward to David in 1 Chronicles 11:17. The Philistines have taken control of David's homeland of Bethlehem and he is in a stronghold.

Read the above passage and fill in the blanks:

"And David said longingly, 'Oh that someone would give me _____ from the _____ in Bethlehem that is by the gate'"

Sister, you may be in a stronghold, feeling like you are surrounded by the enemy or longing for an easier life. If that's the situation you find yourself in right now, I know you can relate closely with the words of David.

Growing up as a shepherd in Bethlehem there would have been moments of isolation where David longed for the days when life was easier and days were slower. I can sympathize with him in his longing for home. Perhaps you've relocated due to work, military, or out of necessity.

REFLECTION:

Don't you have moments where you long for a special location that is near to your heart? Where might that be for you?

When I was a little girl bodies of water spoke to my heart. It didn't matter if it was a lake nearby or the ocean that touched my toes during a family vacation. Water called to me and I sang to it. Innocence as a child wraps you in a cloak of bliss and allows you to dream, imagine and wonder. Moments beside water cause me to dream.

Today that little girl filled with innocence is long gone. One thing that remains unchanged is being pulled towards water.

I often wonder if women of the Bible had that same pull. I sit here and type alone in the woods and wonder if you sweet reader feel that same magnetic pull towards water.

Keith and I make our home in Charleston, South Carolina, which is a place with many beautiful beaches. Additionally we are also four hours away from the Blue Ridge Parkway and the gorgeous Smoky Mountains. In fact, this Sunday morning that is exactly where I'm sitting. I can hear the trickle of a waterfall and it caused me to set my book aside and wander. We have spent the last week camping in the forest and as we've hiked, if I hear the sound of the water, I instinctively walk towards it.

Was it the same way for women of the well? They wouldn't have been able to hear the trickle of the waterfall or the sounds of the forest. Did the water call to them? I wonder if the well called to them in a way water calls to us? If so, let's explore the roots of that wonder and wander a bit together shall we?

In our intro today we chatted about Cinderella and fairy tales of girls with longings going to the well. Whether you've traveled to Italy or to a fountain in your local mall or town square, no doubt you've leaned over and noticed coins scattered at the bottom. Our dreams and wishes are brought to the fountains and to wishing wells. I'll never forget my first trip to Disney. I was 34 years old and already had found my prince and my Prince, but something in me had to meet Cinderella and I had to find her wishing well.

Going to Disney had been a lifelong dream and on our second wedding anniversary, my prince made it a reality for me. When I turned the corner of Main Street at Disney World, I saw her castle for the first time and my eyes filled with tears. Magic. It was kisses from my childhood and memories of dress up and fairy tales. I approached her castle, stood in line with my husband to meet Cinderella and have my picture taken with her. As I stood behind three very small little girls, I saw her. Dressed in her beautiful blue dress, black head band, and perfectly coiffed blonde hair, she looked exactly like Cinderella. Wrapped up in Disney magic, she was Cinderella. My eyes once again filled with tears and the little girls in front of me turned around and said "Mommy, why is she crying". I immediately felt the ridiculousness of my emotions and I'm confident I turned blood red. Before I could restore my composure, it was my turn and I stepped up to meet her. At that point I was full on crying. Let me tell you sister, I couldn't speak through the tears, and this Cinderella was graceful, staying completely in character.

She asked me "Is this your first time in my kingdom?" I nodded through my ridiculous tears. She pressed further attempting to engage this blubbering 30 year old woman

"What has been your favorite part so far". Through my tears, all I could to respond was point at her.

Here was her response: "Me?" She pulled both her hands together clasping them close to her heart. "Well, I don't know if you know this, but I have been waiting a very long time for you to come and visit me. I have something very special to share with you. If you go just outside my castle, you'll find where we keep the horses. Now listen very carefully. If you go out there and you look closely, you'll find a beautiful white horse with a blue ribbon tied to it. That is my horse and was a wedding present to me from the Prince. Go out and ride her. I know you'll love it".

It was magical. It was make believe, and I knew in my mind that I was being ridiculous but something about that magic and the longings, dreams and my childhood mixed together in that moment that overrode my practical 30 year old brain.

Let me just tell you, I married a prince. I truly did. He was in tears watching my childhood dreams come true. After our time with Cinderella, he led me by the hand and took me straight to the carousel. We walked around and around looking for the white horse with the blue ribbon. We searched until the carousel started turning to which I grabbed the horse closest to me and jumped up on top. A Disney employee walked by and I leaned over to him and said, "I know this is ridiculous, but can you please tell me which one is Cinderella's horse?". He looked at me, looked around and then looked back up, "You're on it". I looked back, and sure enough, by the horse's tail was a painted blue ribbon. I looked back at him and with a big smile I said "Now that was magic".

Wishing wells. Magic. Singing in a forest. These are the things of our heart as women. It's vital to who we are. I watch today my nieces dress up as princesses, sing, twirl, and perform made up plays for us and I delight in it because these are moments where they find the magic of being a female. The purity and joy of being delighted in.

Tucked vitally into our childhood is the wishing well. Somewhere along the way we have identified that the well is the source of where our dreams begin to come true.

Moments of magic. Moments of longing. Moments of memories. These are all cause for us to stop, slow down, push aside the rush or tasks of the day ahead of us, and sit to reflect. Tucked deep within these memories is the source of who we are and the language of our heart. Let's listen.

Day Three: Digging Our Well

"And the Lord will guide you continually and satisfy your desire in scorched places and make your bones strong"

Isaiah 58:11

PRAY ALOUD AND ASK THE LORD TO OPEN YOUR EYES TO THE TRUTH HE HAS WAITING FOR YOU, AND ASK HIM TO TUNE YOUR EARS TO HEAR HIS VOICE.

Bible Reading: John 7: 37- 39

Yesterday we defined six important and vital elements to the construction and life of a well.

List them below:

1. _____
2. _____
3. _____
4. _____
5. _____
6. _____

Today we're going to construct your well. So grab your coffee, your red pen and let's dig deep.

Before we know where to dig, we need to identify what we're digging for.

In ancient Middle East, they were digging for _____.

Water was a life source as we mentioned yesterday. Without it life (be it human, plant or animal) wouldn't survive.

Apart from Christ, what are a few people, places or things that bring you life?

The only true Source of life is the one name that belongs above any other name: Jesus Christ. Our hearts may long for a husband, a friend, children, parents, health or security, but if we dig down deeper, past the surface levels, we will find that we'll only hit water when we dig deep enough, down into the place where the source bubbles up and it is a source that never dries.

Territorial Boundaries - Choosing Our Land & Building Our Home

In the ancient middle east, property ownership was established in a much different way. Today we engage realtors, lawyers, and contracts to purchase land. In the days of Abraham however if land was unoccupied, it would be up for grabs. Your choice of land would become your territory.

This is the place where you choose to establish your settlement. On this tract of land you set up your tent (home), keep your flocks (work), and the place you raise your family. The one element that hasn't changed is a desire for the best location. Waterfront property is always most desirable in nearly every culture on earth, however in this case, setting your home near a place that was likely to have an abundance of potential for wells would be a desirable location. We all want our homes and lives to prosper and you can't have prosperity in a desert without water.

Let's imagine for a moment that you are the Queen of your settlement. Inside the walls lives your family and close friends: It's your world. If we were to walk up to the gates of your settlement what would the sign say to strangers passing by? Would it state as the name of your camp? Would it state what they can expect? Would it lay out the rules?

Below I'd like you to write out the name of your camp:

In addition, I want you to stake your creed. Who are you?

Who lives there?

What is the foundation that your camp is built on?

Turn with me to look at John 7: 37- 39.

Who stood up and spoke: _____

"Anyone who thirsts, let him come to _____ and drink".

1) Whoever believes in _____

2) Out of his heart will flow _____

3) Now He said this about the _____

Sister, it was Jesus who was saying "get ready, I'm about to pour out on you the Spirit who will dwell within you, and Who will be living waters flowing out of your heart".

Hand Dug And Built - It Takes Work

Are you ready to get your hands dirty? We've arrived at our plot of land, and we're ready to pick up our shovels and start digging down deep to unearth the Source of life.

The depth of your well is entirely up to you. That's the beauty of things that are all your own. There's nobody to tell you what to do or how to do it. But if you lean over the well you've dug and if you quiet yourself, you'll hear it. Do you hear it calling you? It's calling you to go deeper.

Sometimes the creation or work itself will speak to you and tell you what it needs to grow.

No matter what depth your well currently is, you are called to dig down deeper. By digging down you'll find more of the Life Giving Source you are looking for. You'll find more of Jesus. You'll find Him in ways you never imagined and each effort made to move further. My going deeper you're excavating yourself. It's not an easy process, but the reward is more than you can imagine because Jesus will reveal Himself in profound ways.

Not only does the depth of your water source affect your own spiritual life, but it also affects those you love who live on the land with you. If the well you dig is the life source of so many precious people, the deeper you dig, the more water will be available to sustain them. This means your strength to nourish, love and pour out on your family won't deplete quite so quickly. As you dig down deeper, your access to water will increase. That's the beauty of digging deep.

You may have a desire to have a deeper well, but digging deep requires consistent excavation of soil. It might mean getting dirty, it might mean sweat, but it will always mean more Water.

Supporting Walls

Not only is it important to dig down deep, but without supporting walls your well will cave in with the first good rain fall. Once your dirt walls are exposed to the smallest bit of moisture and pressure, you'll find the work you've done to dig deep will be caved in.

It's great to have a deep well, but if at the first sign of pressure your walls cave, then all the work to dig as far as you have will be for naught. Our supporting walls are part of our foundation and vital to the life of our well.

Let's look at the Colossians 1:15 - 17

This entire passage is packed full with Truth that runs so deep, we are only seeing the blades of grass on the surface. For now, lets focus on verse 17.

Write this verse in the space below:

Who holds all things together?

Girls, if ever we needed someone to hold up our walls and hold things together, it's Jesus.

GOD MARK: IF JESUS, WHO HOLDS THE ENTIRE UNIVERSE TOGETHER IS YOUR DADDY, AND YOUR DADDY SAYS HE WILL GIVE YOU PEACE THAT GOES BEYOND OUR UNDERSTANDING AND HE WILL BE THE SOLIDER OF YOUR HEART AND MIND, GUARDING IT, WHAT DO WE HAVE TO WORRY ABOUT?

In Isaiah 58:8 let's peak and see what it tells us about the Lord:

> "Then shall your light break forth like the dawn, and your healing shall spring up speedily; your righteousness shall go before you; **the glory of the Lord shall be your rear guard**".

Sisters if we could understand what it meant to have the Glory of the Lord as our rear guard we would be at our door throwing on those shoes of confidence faster than you could say "Nike".

In the Old Testament we're told that the Glory of the Lord surrounded the tabernacle and when it appeared. The people would drop to their knees and put their face to the ground.

Have you ever been outside and watched a storm roll in or seen a tornado from a distance? Imagine that same Force of nature dwelling overtop your home. That's exactly what the Israelites experienced in the desert. It was the glory of the Lord in physical form.

The glory of the Lord is His Personal Presence

That same power exhibited in the heavens will have your back.

Let. That. Truth. Sink. In.

Oh yes, sweet Jesus, oh yes. Be our walls. Be our rear guard.

There's no greater joy or confidence than daily living convinced that you are a treasured and beloved child of Him who holds ALL things together.

HEARING HIS VOICE & WRITTEN IN RED

Day Four: Digging Deeper

"For in Him all things were created, things in heaven and on earth, visible and invisible, whether thrones or dominions or rulers or authorities. All things were created through Him and for Him. He is before all things, and in Him all things hold together."

Colossians 1:16-17

PRAY ALOUD AND ASK THE LORD TO OPEN YOUR EYES TO THE TRUTH HE HAS WAITING FOR YOU, AND ASK HIM TO TUNE YOUR EARS TO HEAR HIS VOICE.

Bible Reading: Colossians 1

Yesterday we made the choice to establish our homes on land where wells can be dug and water can be found. We know that the work of our hands can only go so far if we don't have Him who waters, grows and refreshes our family, work and lives.

Let's continue the construction of our well with the final steps.

Sealed:

Not only do we need Jesus to hold the walls of our well in place, but we also need His Hand to seal our work brick by brick.

If our walls were established one brick on top of another, it's a matter of science that the water which fills our well would seep out and back into the earth if we don't have something to seal it.

Just outside the walls of our heart we live in a world filled with sponges attempting to draw out of us until we're bone dry and empty. Media, negativity from friends or neighbors, the news, the list goes on and on. It's a parched, dry desert out there. That's the thing about a leak, sometimes you won't even know it exists until it's caused devastating effects.

Now I'm not saying that we don't need to pour out to others. If that were the case, we'd dig our well deep, throw a rock on the top of the hole, and call it a day. Job done, smack our hands together, and go back to bed. No. We were called to pour out to others and love how Jesus loved.

However there's a huge difference between pouring out intentionally vs. pouring out unintentionally.

Think about a time when you poured out intentionally:

Now think about a time you poured out unintentionally and describe the difference below:

Have you ever cared for someone (physically or mentally) outside of your children or your husband? I would wager to say that you had expectations about the sacrifice that was going to be required of your time and resources. During that time, did you ever take a step back and realize that you were pouring out dangerous amounts that threatened your priorities?

We're called to pour out and to give to others. In fact, God equips us for such a calling, which is why He is constantly filling us up when we go to our well. But we were never meant to be drained by leaks in our walls.

In that same way, the care of this crazy world we live in can also barrel towards us like a tsunami, crashing all those carefully built walls. We neither want to live in a place where we're totally drained or overwhelmed with our walls caving in.

Protected

Not only is the sealant a vital element to our well, but it is also critical to protect the water from contamination from the outside.

This Truth could be an entire day of study in and of itself. Girls, Satan is a creeping crawling, nasty microcosm that wants to infest, pollute, and contaminate what God is filling in and through us. However God is our Rock and our refuge.

Read Genesis 29: 1 - 3

What was placed on top of the well:

Record The Truth You Find In The Following Verses:

Psalms 78: 35 -

2 Samuel 22: 3 -

2 Samuel 22: 32 -

How can you apply the truth about the rock on top of the well with the above verses to your own life?

From the Old Testament to the New Testament the Lord is referred to as our Rock. The rock placed on top of the well would have been there for 4 primary purposes:

    1) The well wouldn't fill up with sand as the wind blew.

    2) From being misused by others

    3) It signified that it belonged to an owner

    4) To keep it pure from contamination.

Ladies, the same way God is that very rock for us:

    1) He protects us from life overwhelming and burying us:

2) He protects us from enemy attacks.

3) His Presence as our Rock sets us apart as His and His ownership on our lives.

4) His Presence protects us from predators who try to contaminate our spiritual life.

Clinging to the God of Abraham, Isaac and Jacob as our Rock and allowing Him to seal us up, guard us and protect that which He is doing in our life and hearts is vital to keeping the enemy out.

Emotional Ties:

Read II Sam. 23:14 - 17

We briefly looked at this same story of David in day two, but it's worth revisiting and digging a little deeper. David had been removed from his comfortable palace walls and at this moment in Scriptures he was hiding in caves. I love moments in the Bible when we see heroes of our faith have moments of "realness". Hiding deep within a cave while his enemies occupied his homeland, he let his mind wander and drift towards days of his childhood when life was easier, days were calm and routine was something that could be counted on. He let his thoughts escape through his lips in verse 15.

What did he long for?

What was the response of his mighty men?

What was David's Response?

Have you ever had a moment where you longed for easier times? Have you ever wished you could return to the home you grew up at? Many of us have a place we call "back home". It can easily become the place where we forget all the negative and only remember it with fond memories. No matter where we live, there's no doubt whatsoever that life is hard. When the pressure mounts and troubles seem to multiply, it's easy to start dreaming of days when things were easier. That's exactly what David did.

What are a few things in your life right now that are making you long for quiet days?

David thought back to days as a shepherd boy, where he spent his time with the flocks, and bringing them to the well near Bethlehem to water the sheep. No doubt this was a place where he met his friends, laughed. It was a time when life was easy. As a shepherd boy there was no palace waiting for him to rescue, no sworn enemies seeking his life. Things were simple.

Sometimes the well signifies our desire to go back to easier times. The well is our safe haven.

Laying Down Our Shovels:

Girls, as we wrap up today's lesson I want you to write below a recap of how the Lord spoke to your heart today. We covered a lot of areas and I hope you started today's study in prayer asking the Lord to speak to you clearly. If you picked up that red pen, I'd encourage you to glance over today and recap it in the space below. We don't want to miss anything the Lord is telling us or asking us to do.

As we close let's hold onto this truth: Any effort put in will become precious to you. That which you pour in, more will be poured out. Your well will be a sacred place for you.

You can't come dry to the well and expect it to overflow. Fullness is not measured by what's contained, but by what is pouring up and over the top.

HEARING HIS VOICE & WRITTEN IN RED

Day Five: Defining Our Purpose

"Jacob's well was there; so Jesus, wearied as he was from his journey, was sitting beside the well. It was about the sixth hour. A woman from Samaria came to draw water..."

John 4: 6 -7

PRAY ALOUD AND ASK THE LORD TO OPEN YOUR EYES TO THE TRUTH HE HAS WAITING FOR YOU, AND ASK HIM TO TUNE YOUR EARS TO HEAR HIS VOICE.

Bible Reading: Isaiah 54

Discipline is not something I enjoy. My husband and I own a couple of businesses and the demands keep our schedules very full. I've tried time blocking, but there's something that feels restraining in that. As a creative, I tend to enjoy being motived and inspired towards work. This is a gift but it can also be a detriment. If I waited until inspiration struck, I'd likely never finish a project. There is one thing that I am very disciplined about and that's carving out time in my day (preferably early in the morning) to draw away and spend some time with Jesus and reading my Bible.

When I first began this routine of daily reading my Bible it was out of sheer desperation. It was a very low period in my life. I had just left my fiancée; a man I had been with for 7 years. He wasn't my husband, but we were living together.

Life should have been very good at this point. He was an important figure and an elected official in the Government of Canada, and an established businessman and lawyer. We lived a big life with multiple homes, vehicles and extravagant trips around the world. On the weekends we would spend our time out on our boat, or catching a train to Quebec City or Montreal for some shopping. During the week my only job was to keep the house clean and prepare for the next social function.

In 2007, I distinctly recall walking into the doctor's office, sitting down and having him tell me that I was a sitting duck for depression (if I wasn't already there). His plan of attack was me losing weight, exercising, and finding purpose or he was going to put me on medication.

Bare in mind that I was a Christian and had been since childhood, despite my life not looking that way. It wasn't until out of sheer desperation that I agreed to start a Bible Study very similar to this one, that I realized I had spent my entire life missing out on the benefits of being a daughter of the Most High God. The Bible Study I was doing was a 12 week study. By week 6, God had grabbed my heart so tightly and gave me a taste of what could be. I left my fiancée, moved back to my folks, and started all over again with God.

Those days moving back home at the age of 27 were very humbling. I had no vehicle (I had sold my car and was driving one of his fancy ones), and very few belongings. The day I returned home, I got off my flight and immediately went to a ladies Bible Study. I knew I wouldn't last a minute without staying so plugged into Scripture and tucked under Jesus's arm. This is the moment in life when I learned something about the Holy Spirit as well. He's a gentleman. He never pushes, He always gently guides. For me His gentle touch at the small of my back couldn't have been more real if He had physically touched me as He intentional guided me home.

It was in these quiet, lonely moments that each morning I would roll out of bed, grab my coffee and dive into Study with Jesus. There I found He met me every single time, and I hung on His every word. It was in those quiet moments of heart break that I met Jesus in a way I had never imagined. I had been taught the principles of his personality, but being Face to face with Him was an entirely different matter. It's in these precious moments that my discipline to wake up every morning and have my quiet time with Him turned into an anxious expectation because I knew He was waiting for me.

Each morning during those precious months of recovery has continued more than a decade later. I come to the well to meet with Him, He pours out on me Living Water, and I come away refreshed.

Write Acts 3:20 in the space below:

Plumbing wasn't a luxury that our sisters in the Bible would have been afforded. Every morning or each evening they were required to make the trek out to the well to gather the days water for themselves and for their families. I like to think that not only was it important to make their journey to the well in the morning or at the end of the day to save themselves from the heat, but they must have also enjoyed that quiet walk as the earth was waking up, or as the quiet of evening set in.

The distance between the homes and the well itself would have varied from one settlement to another. To have had a well located directly inside the walls of your settlement would have been a luxury. The distance to travel to and from the well, along with the weight of the water on your shoulder would have been far easier than the less-fortunate communities. More commonly, the women would have been required to leave the city and walk out to the place where the well would have been located.

It's important to note that water was available to every individual of that community. As a citizen you would have been afforded the right to access that water.

Not only was water a necessity to life, but it also required being intentional to step out of their homes. There wasn't a day where the women would have lounged on their chair with their cup of coffee and questioned whether or not they felt like gathering water. They knew that to not gather water would mean certain death to them.

What are some things you could do to be intentional about going to your well?

Applied Truth:

Earlier this week we identified the water in our well as the Holy Spirit. Morning by morning His mercies are new and waiting for us. It doesn't take a seasoned veteran in the faith to tell us that if we spend time away from the Presence of the Most High that our hearts will shrivel like bacon in a frying pan.

Have you ever gone through a dry period in your marriage or in an important relationship? Let's just be real. We all have. Have you ever noticed what a game changer it can be to intentionally sit down, look into each other's eyes and talk? It can tear down walls, encourage, mend wounds, and strengthen our covenant. That same principle applies with Jesus.

Knowing that He is there waiting for you to draw yourself away from your phone, your schedule and your demands to just sit at the table and dialogue with Him, is the sweetest invitation. He's flexible and eager. There's no condemnation or judgement. There's no rigid schedule you have to follow. Just the sweet kindess of Jesus eager to speak with you.

Admittedly I've tried living life out of dry faith. I totally agree that we're supposed to live out a consistent, daily, sacrificial life which includes faith, but we were not meant to live a life of dry faith.

I can personally attest to this truth: When you stop looking at your time and relationship with Jesus as another thing to mark off your to do list and you start looking at it as a time to sit down and bask in the Presence of your Husband, it changes everything.

Now before you start get all bristly about me being irreverent about God, **I want you to turn to Isaiah 54:5. In fact I want you to write it out below and instead of writing it word for word, I want you to make it personal by adding your name in the verse:**

Marriage is used throughout Scripture as a parallel drawn between God and the church (not the buildings, the people) and a man and his wife. In fact, there are numerous Scriptures that indicate that God looks at the body of believers (that means you) as His bride.

Even the most pious, strict, God fearing woman would struggle to live in a loveless, dry marriage. Of course it's not all rainbows and fairy tale walks in the woods. It's a battle. It's hard. We daily fight for love. What if we started looking at our relationship with Jesus similar to the way we look at our marriages?

For those of you who are single, this is going to be life in your bones. I was unmarried until I turned 30 years old and let me tell you, I relied on this truth and lived it out practically. The Lord my Husband is my Maker. He is a comforter, protector, provider, counsellor, and yes even lover. Some of the most intimate moments of my life have been moments when Divine Love swept down and did something so profound that it was like a kiss. More on that later.

Married or unmarried, every single day we need to be intentional about leaving our household tasks and stepping out to come to the well and meet the Lord. We require water. Did you realize that in the best case scenario, you can only survive 8 - 10 days at best without it? Given a harsh climate you're likely to survive 3 days at best. Girls, we live in a very harsh environment. Arrows from the enemy are constantly being thrown our way. They are camped outside of our settlements like rabid dogs waiting to destroy.

If you've never experienced a fulfilling and soul satisfying quiet time, I want to give you a couple of tips that I think will take your quiet time to the next level.

1) Set a time.

This is important. Let your Husband your Maker know that He is important enough to be a priority. Make an appointment and stick to it. This will be especially helpful until you begin to know and experience for yourself the depth of intimacy that's waiting to be found with Him. I want to encourage you and suggest you're already half way there. You're holding this study in your hands.

2) Set a space:

I'm going to guess that if you're married with children, you and your husband retreat away from family life to have quality time together. In the same way, if you're dating nothing compares with a quiet dinner sitting across from each other with phones put away and having heart to heart conversation.

The same is true of Jesus. Set a space just for the two of you where you can be alone and uninterrupted as you talk together.

3) Pray First:

Let Him know you're there to talk. Say good morning. Smile. Let Him know you're not coming with an agenda. Don't open your Bible looking for versus to answer the biggest question in life. Just come open to talk about whatever He wants to talk about. Of course dialogue goes both ways, and you can bring Him all your troubles, but also come intentionally just to sit before Him.

4) Worship:

Ambiance. It's the reason the violinist in the fancy restaurants are so cliché. Nothing sets the tone like music. When you come before Him and you sing to Him, you're going to find it's much easier to step into that quiet space with Him.

5) Read:

I'm a huge proponent for working through Bible Study books as you're getting started. Pick a teacher you enjoy and work through each lesson day by day. It's one reason I wanted this piece of writing to be in the form of a Bible Study rather than a book. A Bible Study will help guide you to places of truth in Scripture. It's been my experience that sometimes the Spirit will speak to me from passages nearby where the study was leading me. To be clear, the study may lead me to one page, but the Spirit has plans for my eyes to dart to the opposite side of the page where He's going to speak clearly to my heart.

6) In the quiet:

It's amazing what we can hear when we stay quiet long enough to listen. If we can quiet ourselves down to give Him a chance to get a Word in, we might be amazed at what He's willing to unlock and share with us.

Girls, just as we talked about the depth of our well-being dependent on how deep we want to dig, the same is true with our marriages. If we want a vibrant marriage, it's critical we invest in quality time and effort to plug into our husbands and not let distractions of households and life get in the way of that intimacy. The same is true with Jesus. The more you invest, the more intimacy will be waiting for you.

Let's close with a couple verses I want you to linger over. If you feel the Lord speaks to your heart through some of these verses, then I want to encourage you to grab your journal and write them in red.

James 4:8

Hosea 2:14

Isaiah 54

Psalms 46:5

WEEKLY RECAP

Week 2 - Stories From The Well

Day One: Isaac & Rebekah - Radical Faith Part 1

"By faith Abraham obeyed when he was called to go out to a place that he was to receive as an inheritance. And he went out, not knowing where he was going."

Hebrews 11:8

PRAY ALOUD AND ASK THE LORD TO OPEN YOUR EYES TO THE TRUTH HE HAS WAITING FOR YOU, AND ASK HIM TO TUNE YOUR EARS TO HEAR HIS VOICE.

Bible Reading: Hebrews 11: 8-19

We've arrived at our first story from the well. This one happens to be my favorite love story from the Bible. You would expect that our hero and heroine meet at the well and that's where the magic occurs, but it starts long before that. It all starts with one man believing in something so crazy that it caused him to laugh. It starts with radical obedience, it ends with true love and so much more. Let's get started.

Read Genesis 12: 1 - 4

Often times what we are seeking is rarely where we think to look for it. The same is true of love, of satisfaction, peace, and authenticity. If we jumped straight to the part of this story where the boy meets the girl, we would miss 5 kinds of truth that has the power to radically change the way we think about Jesus, our faith and our own lives weaved into it.

In our Genesis passage we find one man, a conversation and an action. Outline it below:

Man:

The conversation was with who?

What was told?

What occurred?

Let's lock on these words in verse 1 and verse 4:

"Go" (verse 1), "So Abram went" (verse 4).

There's such purity and beauty in this story and it all stems from one word: Obedience.

O·BE·DI·ENCE

NOUN "COMPLIANCE WITH AN ORDER, REQUEST, OR LAW OR SUBMISSION TO ANOTHER'S AUTHORITY"

In this passage God isn't asking Abram to go to Lowes and get a hammer and come home.

He is asking Abram to leave his home and his family to "a land that I will show you". Does that make your heart beat faster like it does mine?

When I was 11 years old, God asked my father to leave his country, and our family and to go to a place where the road literally stopped (it was that far north). It was devastating to leave family behind and all that was familiar, but at least we knew where we were going, we knew the assignment (start a church and love the people). Absolutely this experience required faith on behalf of my parents. There was faith in the initial "yes" and then there was faith each and every time things got tough. That's continuous faith.

For Abraham, he was given a command without a destination. Now, perhaps it's my controlling nature (I admit that's something that I struggle with) but I love to know a plan. If I know the plan and details I'm all in. In my mind I can really get behind it and more fully support if I know the end game. That's not faith. Faith is one foot in front of another when you have no idea where you're going. Abram's faith was activated the moment he moved his foot when his heart said yes.

The secret to a life of faith is that it is always a continual "yes" that's followed by action. Let's look at his ongoing radical faith in the following actions. **Record them below:**

Genesis 13:18 –

Genesis 17:26 –

Genesis 22 –

When we opened our study today we found a man who heard from the Lord, and followed in blind obedience to what God had told him. We see that he and his wife were barren and old in age. By the power and Word of the Lord they conceived a child (Isaac).

That treasured promise had to be given back to the Lord on an altar, knowing that even if Abraham had to go through with killing his beloved child that God could bring him back to life.

Radical. Faith. When we set aside the rules, regulations and religion, we have relationship. God asked Abram to go, and he did. From that first step of obedience, Abram and God began to have a relationship where they talked together as friends, and Abram literally negotiated with God (Gen. 18: 22- 33). They spoke Face to face.

Would Abraham sacrifice the son he had waited for so long when his relationship with God was new? I can speak from personal experience that the steps of faith the Lord has asked me to make recently, I could have never done when I was new to my relationship with Jesus. Faith is a muscle that builds over time, and relationship is the fuel that keeps it moving.

There was something important that God told Abram in the beginning of this journey, and as we did our reading, we skimmed over it. Did you catch it? There are 6 promises.

Let's record them below (Genesis 12:2-3):

1)

2)

3)

4)

5)

6)

Let's tie you into this story. Note the last sentence of verse 3. "In you all the families of the earth shall be blessed".

Look at Galatians 3:29 with me below:

"And if you are Christ's, then you are Abraham's offspring, heirs according to the promise."

Get. A Hold. Of That! If you are a follower of Christ, then you are a descendant of Abraham, and as such the promises delivered to Abraham from the mouth of God become yours to not just hold onto, but to cling to with all your might. It becomes your home. To be blessed and to in return be a blessing. He will fight for you and be your rear guard.

Today we've travelled a long way together and we've searched through a lot of scripture and our search for the well is still some ways off, but the truths from today is the land on which our well is found. We will never be full and overflowing unless we build our well on the ground of obedience. Obedience to His plan. To His voice. To His heart.

Make It Personal & Consider It:

What is one thing in your heart you know God has called you to do that will require faith to walk it out?

To move forward in obedience, what is your next step?

If nothing immediately comes to mind, take heart. Ask the Lord what He wants you to do and the next step of faith that should be taken. Remember that all we ask of Him is "yes and amen" (II Cor. 1:20). Without having faith with legs, it's impossible to please God (Hebrews 11:6).

HEARING HIS VOICE
& WRITTEN IN RED

Day Two: Isaac & Rebekah - Faith That Doesn't Wait (Part 2)

"Before I had finished speaking in my heart, behold, Rebekah came out with her water jar on her shoulder...."

Genesis 24:45

PRAY ALOUD AND ASK THE LORD TO OPEN YOUR EYES TO THE TRUTH HE HAS WAITING FOR YOU, AND ASK HIM TO TUNE YOUR EARS TO HEAR HIS VOICE.

Bible Reading: Genesis 24

Today we're going to cover the entire chapter of Genesis 24. You can go ahead and read the chapter in full or we can work through it together. Let's get started.

This is a longer passage but a beautiful one. Be sure to be in a quiet place. If you feel or see a verse jump off the page at you be sure to record it in your journal in red. The purpose of the verse doesn't need to make sense at the time, just record it in faith.

There was something big at stake. A promise. A promise that would not only change one couple's barren life, but a promise that would extend down through the generations to where you sit today. Strict adherence to the Word of the Lord was of upmost importance. In fact, it was critical. God blesses obedience, and Abraham's life was living proof.

Let's look at chapter 24, verses 1 - 4.

Verses 1 through 4 allows us to pull back the door of Abraham's tent and have an intimate look at Abraham's deathbed, last recorded words and the thoughts that lay heavy on his mind as he's lying there awaiting death. One commentary said it best, "Abraham enters history through the divine promises (12:1-3,7); he passes out of history with this promise on his lips". *(Matthews, 2005)*

In all Abraham's wisdom from the years of living out his relationship with God, He lived in the reality that without obedience to the spoken Word of the Lord, all that would be promised would be lost. Not only was it critical to a father to pass down his physical genes, Abraham knew that without a spouse who would share the same belief in God, Isaac would be set up for failure in his pursuit to live a life of obedience for God.

> *"Take care, lest you make a covenant with the inhabitants of the land to which you go, lest it become a snare in your midst...and you take of their daughters for your sons, and their daughters whore after their gods and make your sons whore after their gods".*
>
> *Exodus 36:12,16*

Going back to chapter 24 and verses 2-4, this is an odd scene that doesn't translate well for us. Abraham's servant is called to fill one last wish from his master and he asks to make a covenant with him. The servant places a hand under Abraham's thigh. As awkward as it is, by placing a hand under Abraham's thigh, he would have been essentially touching his genitals. Let's explain the significance of this.

By swearing an oath or covenant with the servant, he is in fact imitating the act between himself and God. Furthermore by the servant placing his hand where he did, he is touching the very place the circumcision would have taken place, which had been a sign he physically wore to bear witness to the oath God had made with him (Gen. 17).

The oath was also critical because Isaac needed a wife to produce children and thereby carry out the promises of God. One commentary that I had read noted the parallel between the oath being made with the hand of the servant set at the place of reproduction, and the matter of reproduction being at stake in order to receive the promise of the Lord.

This request was a serious one in nature. Abraham had been active his entire life to be responsive to the Lord in obedience, but laying in his deathbed required him to be dependent on his servant, and trust that he would carry out his last requests.

At this point I'm feeling sorry for that servant. He had stood by the sidelines and watched the face of God speak to Abraham. He knew from the buzz around the camp fire of interactive relationship Abraham had with the Most High God. He was now being called on to be Abraham's proxy, act on his behalf.

And just like that, we've arrived at our first moment at the well.

Let's take a peak and look at Genesis 24: 10 - 15.

Did you catch the first 5 words of verse 15?

Write it below:

Abraham could reassure his servant that God would go before him and that his prayer would be heard "before he had finished speaking", because he knew from past experience that God was indeed interested in the details of his life. This is a truth that I've only recently really knit into my heart and allowed to change the way I approach each day.

What is one thing in your life that you would like for God to be intimately involved with?

What if He already is? If we could have eyes to see the invisible, I wonder what we would see behind the stage, past the curtain of your life. We would be amazed at how he's weaving events, people, and situations together to bring this thing to fruition. I'd wager we would be dumbfounded if we only knew what he was doing just behind the veil.

What would our reality look like and how would we live life differently if we knew that there were times when before we even finish speaking, God is answering us?

Read verses 16 - 21.

Let's focus in on Rebekah's response to the servants request for a drink of water. *"She quickly let down her jar"* and gave him a drink, and she *"quickly emptied her jar into the trough and ran again to the well to draw water"*. **Her willingness and her heart became his sign**.

Verse 21 might be one of my very favorites verses in the Bible. It drips with an intimacy and a knowing that he could have confidence in being led moment by moment in the Lord.

"The man gazed at her in silence to learn whether the Lord had prospered his journey or not".

In verses 22 - 56 we see the servant meeting with Rebekah's family and you can almost hear the excitement in his voice at the retelling of God's provision for Abraham and His faithfulness to both Abraham and the servant.

We can learn a lot from Rebekah's story through her responses. We already know that not only did she meet the servant's request, she exceeded it by not only giving him water from the well, but also by taking it upon herself to water his livestock. Let's look at her response after she receives the blessing of her family to marry this man she's never met.

Read verses 55 - 58.

What was Rebekah's response?

Can you imagine having someone show up randomly one day, declaring the will of the Lord is for you to leave your family and marry a man you've never laid eyes on?

Her quick response and compliance not to linger, once again shows her heart and trust. "I will go". Three words of obedience that change the course of history.

In yesterday's journey we found Abraham's response to God's command to leave his family and homeland. His response was to pick up and go. He didn't tarry. He never lingered between obedience and disobedience.

We find that same willingness in Rebekah. Her sincere desire to be obedient to the will of the Lord, despite the upheaval to her physical life was distinctly similar to that of her future father-in-law. I don't know about you, but I'm inspired. I'm inspired by her faith and a willingness to say "yes" without questioning, bartering for more time, or taking a hot moment to consider.

Notice just how quickly both Rebekah and Abraham both say yes to the Lord. Obedience is the immediate action behind a request that. The action is the voice of your faith. It's easy to put off an obedient response to something God is asking you while you contemplate the ramifications. It's also easy to put off while you barter with God. You may tell yourself that you're simply praying to confirm that this is truly the Lord. But girl, let me tell you this: When you know God is asking you to do something, just do it.

Is there something the Lord has been asking you to do that will require you to bend your knee and be obedient to Him? If so, record it below:

This is the one time in life that I want to challenge you to "do now, think later". Radical faith that causes miracles and moves mountains is a faith that says yes and responds in action and thinks later.

Go ahead and finish reading verses 59 - 67, and enjoy the romance of it.

Perhaps one of the most beautiful romances and accounts in history, is the story of Rebekah and Isaac. It's interesting to note that the author of Genesis thought so too because it's one of the longest continuous accounts in the entire book.

Abraham was committed to follow exactly what the Lord told him. The yes of Rebekah's heart caused her to take radical action in obedience to the Lord. Because of those agreements with the Divine plan we have verses.

> *"Isaac lifted up his eyes and saw.... (vs 63), and when "Rebekah lifted up her eyes, and when she saw Isaac (vs. 64).*

There's something beautiful, pure, and mysterious in this story. It all began from two obedient hearts.

Close today by asking the Holy Spirit what He wants you to say to you.

HEARING HIS VOICE & WRITTEN IN RED

Day Three: Jacob & Rachel: The Not So Perfect Fairy Tale

"As he looked, he saw a well in the field, and behold, three flocks of sheep lying beside it, for out of that well the flocks were watered...Then Jacob kissed Rachel and wept aloud"

Genesis 29: 2, 11

PRAY ALOUD AND ASK THE LORD TO OPEN YOUR EYES TO THE TRUTH HE HAS WAITING FOR YOU, AND ASK HIM TO TUNE YOUR EARS TO HEAR HIS VOICE.

Bible Reading: Genesis 29: 1 - 20

It was the morning of my dear sister's wedding and she was a woman on a mission. There was no keeping up with her as she made her way to the preacher bound and determined to speak with him regarding one very important last minute instruction: "Do not make me say the word 'obey' in our wedding vows". I love her wild and feisty heart.

If you read the traditional vows, you'll note the woman commonly says:

"I, (Bride), take thee, (Groom), to be my wedded Husband; to have and to hold from this day forward, for better for worse, for richer or poorer, in sickness and in health; to love, cherish, and to **OBEY**, till death us do part, according to God's holy ordinance; and thereto I give thee my troth."

Obedience in our culture today is perceived as a negative word. One that brings thoughts of servitude, submission (in the negative sense) and being a door mat. In fact it's interesting to note the use of the word in our daily language, as compared to that of the use in the 1800's.

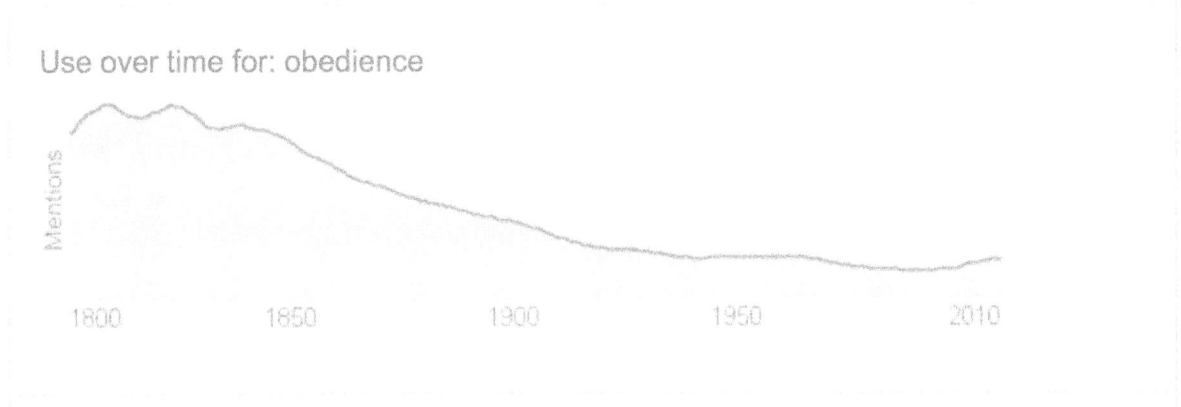

It's not far reaching to summarize that the deterioration of society stems from our breakdown of the family unit. As seen above the further we moved from using (and acting on) the word 'obedience', our society gradually began to deteriorate to gun violence in schools, drug addicts overdosing in the car with their toddlers and sex slave trafficking at an all-time high.

We pick up our second story of the well with Isaac and Rebekah's son, Jacob. But to understand the scene at the well and their love story, we need to journey back to the home of Jacob and look at his family life.

Read Genesis 25:21, compare the similarity between Rebekah and Sarah below:

A continuous theme we're going to see as we journey through our stories from the well is this: A woman with unmet longings in her heart always results in catastrophic damage with collateral impact that is wide spread.

My personal story was one of a complete train wreck on the track of loneliness and emptiness until the very day the Lord ordained for me to meet my husband. Once married the reality that I wouldn't have my own children hit me like a brick. I had been a child who stuffed pillows under her shirt and pretended she was pregnant and then subsequently handled and carried my 'babies' around with care. The result of that perceived lack turned into attempting to self-fulfill in any way that I could with anyone that I could. A certifiable, front cover train wreck.

Although those in the Bible lived in a different time with a very different culture, let's not lose the reality that they were very much humans filled with the same desires, same ambition, and same sin nature as we have.

Perhaps it's because Abraham was such a giant of the faith and a man who spoke to God face to face as a friend, that his son (Isaac) turns into a grown man who is extremely passive. In fact, one of the only places in Scripture that we'll find him taking the initiative of activity is in verse 21 as we read above, when he prayed to God on behalf of his wife.

In **Genesis 25: 22** we find that the children (twins) in her womb struggled together within her. In fact during the pregnancy, she was in such agony she wished for death. During the birth itself the younger (Jacob) clung to the heel of the older (Esau).

Read Genesis 25: 23 - 34 and answer the following questions:

1) The prophesy given to Rebekah stated that there were 2 _____ in her womb.

2) Esau was a skilled _____ (vs. 27)

3) Jacob was a _____

4) **The parents (Isaac and Rebekah) had their favorites record the details below:**

5) **Record the scenario between Esau and Jacob (verses 29 - 34).**

6) **What do we learn about Jacob:**

7) **What do we learn about Esau:**

Not only did Esau barter his brother for his birthright over a bowl of stew (that must have been some stew), but we also see a devilish and manipulative plan to trick his ailing father into giving him the blessing. It's interesting to note that Jacob's name means "he who cheats".

In the verses we read above, we can plainly see the hostility between the brothers. There's certainly no love lost between the two. In chapter 27 we find that those unmet longings of Rebekah transitioned her from a type of Abraham as we saw yesterday, to a woman who is manipulative and calculating when she sets up a scenario for her favorite son (Jacob) to steal the blessing reserved for the firstborn male.

The family drama increases and this dynamic is clearly ready to burst under the pressure of feud. Under the direction of his family he's sent back to Rebekah's family. Returning to our story is Laban who we met yesterday.

If you recall a servant was sent by Abraham to take a wife for Isaac because there was a strict adherence that Isaac would not return the homeland. It was critical to Abraham that strict adherence and obedience to the Word of the Lord be followed and maintained. Not one foot would be moved from the promise.

At this point in our story we are drawing strong comparisons between Abraham and his son Isaac. Two very different men with a similar goal: finding their son a wife.

The passive nature of Isaac allowed the chaos of the brotherly feud to rule the home, resulting in sin that required Isaac to flee the promise land seeking refuge from his mother's family. Let's be clear – he was heading back to the land that Abraham never wanted his descendants to return to.

Let's step back in time and stand next to Laban as he watches his nephew approach. No doubt we'd turn our heads to look at him and he'd comment on the lack of fanfare. No doubt he keenly remembered the loaded treasures, camels and a display of wealth to be left for Laban in return for Rebekah's hand in marriage. Instead we find poor Jacob with nothing to show but himself and the sandals on his feet.

The purpose of sending Jacob back to Laban was to marry from within the family and to preserve the family (please note the irony here).

Unlike the servant who inquired of God and involved Him in the decision making process and who then acted on his resolve to return immediately to Abraham with the bride, we find a very different scene here with Jacob.

Let's step up to the well and watch the romance unfold in chapter 29: 1 - 20.

Note the initial time spent with Laban: _____ (verse 14).

Record the traits of Leah and her sister Rachel below:

From a passive father who received his wife without having ever laid eyes on her and the only record of activity (as we noted before) was a prayer on behalf of his wife that she conceives, we find (quite the opposite) an eager Jacob who doesn't think twice about serving 7 years for his bride, Rachel.

Growing up, this was one of my favorite stories because all I saw was the romance and beauty of the story. A hero shows up, her life changes and he willingly serves 7 years for her. I often thought about what happened during those 7 years of courtship. Did they meet at the well for long talks, did they walk the fields and take in the sunsets?

As I've grown older I now wonder if that desire and the passing of time happened so quickly because of love or was it because he wasn't in any rush to return to his home and the bitter hatred of his brother.

Let's journey onward in our timeline and we now find an absolutely bizarre situation that is perhaps best meant for the Jerry Springer show. **Read this account for yourself in 29: 21- 30.**

It wasn't enough that our story began with two brothers at bitter odds, but now we have two very angry sisters entangled in one of the most famous love triangles of all time. Both sisters earnestly desired what the other had.

Leah had: _____ (vs 31)

Rachel had: _____ (vs 30)

Family dynamics are hard. Every family has that one story in its history (past or present) that they would like to shove under the rug, cover up, or neglect to speak about.

Do you have an issue that tears at your family? Share it below if you'd like:

Can you imagine sharing a husband with your sister? That alone is a recipe for complete disaster. In verses 31 - 35 we see a fruitful Leah bearing children on a very regular basis and with each birth she takes the opportunity to name each son with a dig at her sister Rachel.

Record the meanings of each name below:

Reuben: _____

Simeon: _____

Levi: _____

Judah: _____

Issachar: _____ (find this in 30:18)

Zebulun: _____ (find this in 30:20)

Bearing four sons for her husband would surely have placed her in great esteem to not only her husband but all who dwelled within their camp. Each birth would have torn at the heart of Rachel and heaped bitterness onto anger. Again we have another example of a woman with unmet needs who takes it upon herself to self-fulfill.

Record her actions in chapter 30: 1 - 8 and the subsequent meaning of these names:

Dan: _____

Naphtali: _____

When Leah saw that she had stopped bearing sons (as if 4 sons weren't enough), she then sent her own servant Zilpah into Jacob to conceive on her behalf. Truly, does it get any more bizarre than this? **Identify the meanings of the names below:**

Gad: _____ (39:11)

Asher: _____ (30:13)

Finally after innumerable bad choices, God answered Rachel's deepest longings in her heart in His own time, and in His own way and opened her womb (Genesis 30: 22).

Record his name and meaning below:

You may be questioning why we spent so much time to dwell on the names and meanings of all of the children, but up above we find 11 of the 12 tribes of Judah. The 12th son would be born (Benjamin) and result in the death of Rachel during childbirth. What's the significance of the 12 tribes of Judah? We have just witnessed the fulfillment of the promise that God made to Abraham that nations would come from his family line.

So out of this blessed mess, where we do find our life application? Let's find it together.

Write down one dream in your heart that you feel is rooted in a calling from God (this could be at any point in your life, including your childhood):

What circumstance in your life has happened to you, or have you stepped in that you feel has hindered you from your dream:

Blessed one, this is my prophetic word to you:

There is nothing you can ever do to thwart the will of God in your life, apart from completely walking away from Him and never returning. If you have a love for Jesus and seeing His plans unfold in your life, there is nothing that you could do that could deter His plan for your life. There's profound freedom in this truth.

Furthermore there's nothing you can do to have messed it up so badly that God would withdraw that plan for you and pass it to someone else. His grace covers all.

HEARING HIS VOICE & WRITTEN IN RED

Day Four: Hagar, The Story Of The Broken - Part 1

"The angel of the Lord found her by a spring of water in the wilderness..."
Genesis 16:7

PRAY ALOUD AND ASK THE LORD TO OPEN YOUR EYES TO THE TRUTH HE HAS WAITING FOR YOU, AND ASK HIM TO TUNE YOUR EARS TO HEAR HIS VOICE.

Bible Reading: Genesis 16

Yesterday we visited the well and were introduced to Rachel who met Jacob at the well. Today we are stepping back in time and returning to his grandfather, Abraham and someone who out of desperation ran for her life and found herself at the well. Today we meet brokenness.

Allow me to transport us back to the days of Abram and Sarai.

> It was an abnormally warm day in this land of His promise. Sarai peaked her head out of the tent and peered across the land that was as flat as her barren womb. A constant reminder of her failure as a wife and the promise of the Lord that was never fulfilled. He said it would happen, He had told them to "know for certain" and yet nothing had changed. Her empty womb, empty hands, and an empty promise remained. Her eyes scanned towards the animals and there she saw her maid, the beautiful Hagar. Young and beautiful this Egyptian girl had served her faithfully.

It could have been loss, emptiness, or a long held belief that stretches its talons back to childhood, but somewhere in our hearts is the idea that God is withholding from us. We know in our minds the story of the "only begotten Son" who came into the world to die for our sins. Often the lines sit on the page and never penetrate to the deepest parts of our heart of what that means to us and what it says of God's heart. Wordless doubts creep in and we're left with whispers in our ear from the enemy. They may sound something like this:

> "You have to do this yourself". "If you want to get this done, you have to take control". "Don't leave this to God, He's too busy". "Do you really think He heard you?" "Do you

really think He cares?"

> *"What comes into our minds when we think about God is the most important thing about us."*
>
> *A.W. Tozer*

This quote sums up today's lesson, wraps it and puts a bow on it. What we think about God and the way we perceive how He thinks about us is the essence of our lives. Ultimately it can dictate our destiny.

Turn with me to Genesis 3: 1-6

Who spoke to the woman (Eve): _____

Fill in the blanks (vs1):

"Did _____, 'You shall not eat of any tree in the garden'?"

Vs. 5: "For _____ that when you eat of it your _____ and you will _____,

knowing good and evil.

Can you imagine where work being leisurely? A life where you never have to wonder where and when the next paycheck will come? You have no concept of what it means to hurl a mug at your husband's head, because of something ridiculous and insensitive he just said. Animals surround you and frolic without fear around your legs as if you were Cinderella in a Disney movie. And in the cool of the evening, you walk with your husband on your left, and God Himself on your right. Together you talk, share dreams, and wander through a garden so beautiful, it leaves you breathless.

Eve knew this life. She experienced all of this and yet the serpent who was "more crafty than all other beasts of the field" was able to casually and very subtly convince her that the same God who enjoyed evening walks in the Garden with her was the same Person who withheld good things from her.

He may be crafty, but he is incapable of coming up with new ideas. He's been hitting replay on the same scheme from the day Eve walked the earth and continues up to just the other day, when you believed a whisper in your ear that God was withholding from you.

It's time to expose him and his lies.

When Eve chooses to believe the lie of the enemy she shares the forbidden fruit with her husband. This next part is very important.

Genesis 3:17:

"Because you have _____"

Now compare verse 17 with the end of Genesis 16:2:

"And Abram _____"

They listened to the voice of their wives. They listened to the voice of the woman who was focused on her "without". When these two women focused on what they perceived as being withheld from them, they put one foot in front of another, reached out their hand, and extended it to the lies they chose to believe. (Wenham, 1994).

Let's take this a step further and translate it to what this means for us today. When was the last time you took action into your own hands and it failed miserably?

For Eve, the action of giving the fruit to Adam resulted in sin entering the world. Let's slip off our Sunday School shoes and not let the reality of this catastrophic event hit us full force. Think about things that personally effect you because of sin:

If sin never entered the world I would have...

1.

2.

3.

The sin of Eve robbed us of walks hand in hand in the garden with God. The sin of Eve causes pain in childbirth, separation from family, broken hearts, tears, and watching your dearest person in the world being lowered in the ground.

Sin always, always breaks hearts, breaks people, and the effects can affect generations.

Let's look at the sin of Sarai.

Read Genesis 16: 3 - 4 and answer the following questions:

Record what Sarai did:

What resulted:

Ok girls, stick with me here: This is a tough ancient custom to translate into our modern day. I find it hard to believe that the same jealousy that rises up in me at the very thought of another woman near my husband, wouldn't rise up in Sarai. A woman had very little rights in those days, but the one thing she had that would cause her to be esteemed was her husband and the children that subsequently came from that union.

Allowing your maid to go to your husband to conceive on your behalf wasn't uncommon. Consider it an ancient custom of surrogate motherhood. A maid would go into their mistress's husband, conceive and the wife would maintain control over the situation by allowing it. What makes this passage so baffling is that Sarai didn't just have her maid go into her husband (as we saw that Leah and Rebekah did with Jacob yesterday), but she gave her maid to be the wife of Abram.

Let's look closely again at Genesis 16:3:

"..._____, Abram's wife, took Hagar the Egyptian, her servant and _____ Abram, _____"

Let's find this link back to Eve once again. Look at Genesis 3:6

"So when the woman saw that the tree was good for foods and that it was a delight to the eyes, and that the tree was to be desired to make one wise, she took of its fruit and ate, and she also _____ some to her _____ who was with her, and he ate.

Have you ever taken matters into your own hands, manipulated, or controlled a situation that back fired and resulted in casualties? I have. If we're honest we likely all have. We didn't need to go to school to learn the art of manipulation. Sadly we intrinsically learned that skill as a result of Mother Eve's sin in the garden.

Sometimes we can spend so much time analyzing situations and outcomes that we distort reality to make it fit with our over analyzed and very wrong expectations. Catastrophic impact.

This was a pivotal moment in history. By acting on impatience and giving her maid to Abram to be his wife the entire Islamic faith can be tracked back to this very moment. This act of taking your maid and giving her to your husband was simply to provide a surrogate to the barren. We saw this action repeated when we looked at the lives of Rachel and Leah who both used their hand maidens to conceive children for them.

What was Hagar's response to being used in this way (Gen 16:4)?

Pride often enters when we perceive we've been given an upper hand.

Sarai's lack of faith (her action) resulted in a failed attempt to manipulate the hand of God. The resulting response of Hagar towards her mistress was sinful pride. There may be nothing more catastrophic than two sinful women at odds with each other. As I write this study, I know some of you have experienced this firsthand, and likely you are still waiting on wounds of the impact to heal.

Have you in the past or present taken matters into your own hands because of a lack of trust in God? If so, record it below:

Read Genesis 16: 5 -6.

Record Sarah's Action (vs 6):

Record Hagar's subsequent action (vs 6)

The words "dealt harshly" in verse 6 is translated from the Greek word '*anah*'. One commentary I read made this amazing connection. Bear in mind that Hagar was from Egypt as you read this:

> *"The same term is used to describe the suffering endured by the Israelites in Egypt (Gen 15:13, Exodus 1:12). So intolerable was her suffering that she ran away." (Page 9, WBC)*

As I write, I'm wishing I could put fireworks on the page, or sit in front of you, grab your arm in excitement and say "just watch this...." Are you ready? Go with me below to Genesis 16:7-12:

> *"The angel of the Lord found her by a spring of water in the wilderness, the spring on the way to Thur. And he said, 'Hagar, servant of Sarai, where have you come from and where are you going'? She said, 'I am fleeing from my mistress Sarai'. The angel of the Lord said to her, "Return to your mistress and submit to her". The angel of the Lord also said to her, "I will surely multiply your offspring so that they cannot be numbered for multitude.'*
>
> *And the angel of the Lord said to her,*
>
> *"Behold, you are pregnant and shall bear a son. You shall call his name Ishmael, because the Lord has listened to your affliction. He shall be a wild donkey of a man, his hand against everyone and everyone's hand against him, and he shall dwell over against all his kinsmen".*

This conversation is the first record of the word "angel" used in Scripture. However, don't confuse this with an archangel like Michael or Gabriel (the messenger angel), because we will miss a critical point.

Theophany is a term used by Biblical scholars that means "a manifestation of God". Scholars will also use the term Christophany to refer to the manifested Presence of the pre-incarnate Christ.

Let's bring this down and look at how this practically applies to our broken friend, Hagar who is at the spring of water. Christ long before He is born of Mary, is appearing to Hagar at the well and meeting her where she is most broken.

If this truth doesn't get you excited, just wait, because by the end of this study I'm confident you're going to be wanting to run to the nearest person and shake them with excitement.

Here's the beauty of this moment: Although the Angel of the Lord calls her by name, we have no indication that by the end of verse 8, that she has any idea Who is speaking to her.

If she knew Who was speaking to her she would no doubt drop to her face in reverence. Not until He speaks to her, confirms her pregnancy, and gives a promise to her and speaks of what is to come for her child, does she realize Who He is that is speaking to her. This is a powerful truth.

A personal encounter with God and hearing His voice will change your perspective of what's possible. Your reality will align with the expectations of heaven.

"And so she called the name of the Lord who spoke to her, 'You are a God of seeing', for she said, 'Truly here I have seen him who looks after me.' Therefore, the well was called Beer-lahai-roi;.

In this divine moment we find a woman who has been used by her authority figure, given to a man for the purpose of conceiving, conceives, allows sin to embed itself into her heart, and as a result is treated maliciously by her superior.

Betrayal. Abandonment. Ridicule. Judgment. Persecution. Humiliation.

She's running home to Egypt as fast as her pregnant feet will carry her and as far from the broken as she can get. While she's running away God meets her at the well.

It is at this well that God calls her by name.

It is at the well that she has a personal encounter.

It is at the well where she confesses her brokenness to Him.

It is at this well that God speaks promises over her.

It is at this well that she learns who God is as a result of a personal interaction with Him.

"You are a God of seeing...."

That same God who speaks face to face as a friend with the patriarch Abraham, a man with power and position is the same Jesus who meets a broken, penniless, servant at a well, and He sees her. *"Truly here I have seen Him who looks after me."*

To be seen. There is a desire nestled so deep, that sometimes we have to tear off layers of the soul to find what we have hidden. The desire remains. It's tucked deeply into our heart if we look hard enough. It's the desire to be seen and to be known.

Perhaps this is why being left by someone you love is so excruciatingly painful. When someone who knows you and has been allowed to truly see deep recesses of your heart walks away, it's almost as if we lose a part of ourselves.

I'm convinced based on experience that when you allow someone to truly see who you are in your rawest moments they become knit into your soul. There's no pain like the pain of being fully known and abandoned by a lover.

This is the story of Hagar and this is my story. Is it yours? If you have picked up this study or it has landed in your lap I firmly believe it is for a distinct purpose. If the story of Hagar has stirred up emotion in you from events that happened decades or days ago, together you and I will walk hand in hand to the well, because as we can see… Jesus is waiting for us.

HEARING HIS VOICE & WRITTEN IN RED

Day 5: Hagar, The Story Of The Broken - Part 2

"Then God opened her eyes, and she saw a well of water..."

Genesis 21:19

PRAY ALOUD AND ASK THE LORD TO OPEN YOUR EYES TO THE TRUTH HE HAS WAITING FOR YOU, AND ASK HIM TO TUNE YOUR EARS TO HEAR HIS VOICE.

Bible Reading: Genesis 21: 1 - 21

Yesterday we stood on the sidelines as Hagar our runaway, pregnant, penniless, servant girl was met by God at a well. That same God who saw every square inch of her heart, was the same God who spoke promises over her and then told her to return to her mistress. She obeys.

TRUTH: If your encounter with God doesn't result in immediate obedience to Him, question the validity of the encounter.

Today we fast forward to chapter 21 and as we walk into Abraham's family once again. We can see it has grown. Sarah has given birth to a son (as promised by God) and called his name Isaac *(21:1-7)*.

In today's reading we see that the camp has gotten noticeably smaller for Abraham's family.

"But Sarah saw the son of Hagar the Egyptian, whom she had borne to Abraham, laughing." Gen. 21:9

The play on words cannot be passed over. Abraham named Isaac in verse 3 and the meaning of the name Isaac is "he laughs". Verse 9 has long been debated by scholars. Some believe that the two boys were playing together and as brothers do, the elder was laughing at the younger (Isaac). Other scholars interpret the word for laughing in verse 9 to mean "mocking". We won't know exactly what Sarah saw as she peered out her tent, but we do know that it caused her to rise up in anger to Abraham and ask him to banish "this slave woman with her son".

Once again we find a similar situation to yesterday's events where Sarah is ignited with fury over a situation she, herself initiated. Her lack of faith and patience for God to accomplish that which He promised is haunting her, not to mention the endless drama that must have been looming over the entire camp for these many years.

Sometimes difficult situations are a result of our own actions. A critical look and then honest self-assessment at how our hand played a leading role in the conflict is rarely something we spend time with. It would require seeing ourselves as less than perfect, calling out areas of our heart that needs the Lord's scalpel and then asking Him to cut. Reacting without taking a moment to own the cause of the crisis causes us not only to look foolish, but ride the downward spiraling train of destruction. Distancing ourselves from the situation doesn't make it go away, it loosens our grip on reality even further.

It's interesting to note that Sarah doesn't refer to Ishmael as "your son" to Abraham (although that's exactly who he is). She's attempting to put as much distance between Ishmael and Abraham as possible by not acknowledging that this is Abraham's son.

Abraham's response is found in verse 11:

> *"And the thing was very displeasing to Abraham on account of his son".*

Let's look up two other situations where a man was *"displeased"* and the resulting actions of such:

To look at the first scenario, we'll have to jump years ahead to a new leader; Moses. He was the man who saw the Lord's chosen people (Israelites) being persecuted by the Egyptians (remember our mention of this yesterday), and subsequently led them out of Egypt towards the promise land. While in the wilderness, God heard their cry and their need for food and gave them food from heaven, manna. The manna was a grain like substance that they could make bread or cakes with.

However, in Numbers 11:10 we see that our word *"displeased"* is used when the people of Israel forget how horrible the persecution was in Egypt and are now complaining about the menu options. The Israelites displeasure in provision (or lack of provision) caused Moses and God to both respond in displeasure.

Our second scenario takes us to I Sam. 18:8. Here we see God's hand-picked a man, who he anointed as King over Israel. This same man become jealous over a young shepherd boy:

> *"As they were coming home, when David returned from striking down the Philistine (Goliath), the women came out of all the cities of Israel, singing and dancing, to meet King Saul, with tambourines, with songs of joy, and with musical instruments. And the women sang to one another as they celebrated, 'Saul has struck down his thousands, and David his ten thousands.' And Saul was very angry, and this saying displeased him." 1 Sam 18:6-7*

Four verses later we find David playing a musical instrument for Saul, and Saul hurling a spear at David's head.

Lessons on where displeasure:

Number 11:10: Displeasure in what God had provided at a specific time and place.

I Samuel 18:8: Jealousy and pride can overtake us and cause us to take actions we never dreamed of.

These two verses seem to sum up the motivations of Sarah.

When we see Abraham was *"displeased"* with Sarah's request to send Hagar and Ishmael away, we can infer that there was a consequential action to her request.

Read Genesis 21:12-14.

Once again we find Hagar on the outskirts of the tent. Only this time, she's not running out of fear, she's being escorted to the outside of the camp and sent away with a child in toe.

Let's chase after and walk with her to see what happens. As you read the passage below, highlight and write in red anything that stands out to you:

> *"...And she departed and wandered in the wilderness of Beersheba. When the water in the skin was gone, she put the child under one of the bushes. Then she went and sat down opposite him a good way off, about the distance of a bowshot, for she said 'Let me not look on the death of the child.' And as she sat opposite him, she lifted up her voice and wept. And God heard the voice of the boy, and the angel of God called to Hagar from heaven and said to her, 'What troubles you, Hagar? Fear not, for God has heard the voice of the boy where he is. Up! Lift up the boy and hold him fast with your hand, for I will make him into a great nation.' Then God opened her eyes, and she saw a well of water. And she went and filled the skin with water and gave the boy a drink.*

And God was with the boy, and he grew up. He lived in the wilderness and became an expert with the bow."

When you're in time of crisis people usually turn one of two ways: Towards God in prayer or against God in disappointment and distrust that can manifest as anger.

As we stand on the sidelines of this scene we see a mother laying her child in the only shade she can find from the burning desert sun. It's hard to wonder why she doesn't cry out to her God of the well, the One she named: El Roi, "He Sees Me". Surely that same God who came and met her face to face at the well would once again meet her here.

Her desperation paralyzes her faith. Look at *who* God heard. It wasn't Hagar crying out for the God she knew, it was young Ishmael who must have cried out to God.

We are people with short term memory problems. God may rescue us in a divine way that causes us to know it was Him and only Him that saved us. Weeks later when the emotion of that situation has passed, we often forget not only the desperation that caused us to cry but we forget the rescuer Himself.

Think back to a time when the Lord rescued you from a situation:

What did you learn about the character and personality of God:

Notice both in this scene and our study yesterday a repetitive act:

God approaches her with a question.

"Hagar, servant of Sarai, where have you _____ and

_____?" (Gen 16:8)

"What _____ you Hagar?" (Gen. 21:17)

Let's also compare one more verse: Look up Genesis 3: 8 - 9.

Record the person who asked, and the question itself below:

One of the reasons I fell in love with studying the Bible is because it's like a treasure hunt. Look at this beautiful treasure hidden just for you:

The name Ishmael means, "God Hears"

The name Hagar gave God, El Roi, means "He sees me".

God in His poetic beauty says this to Hagar in verse 17: *"Fear not, for God has heard the voice of the boy where he is".*

The God Who <u>Sees</u> where the boy lays, has <u>heard</u> the prayer of the boy.

The patience of God is so beautiful. He had already made Himself known to Hagar once before and because she missed it in her moment of desperation, He is so tender to remind her of what He has already shown her.

"Then God opened her eyes, and she saw a well of water..."

His provision was there all along. He just needed to open her eyes to it. A well was waiting. Salvation was waiting. Once again we find our Prince of Peace, Provider, and the One Who sees us intimately showing up at a well and ready to save.

Truth to stand on:

When death has parted you from your loved ones, when you are staring at the back of those who have deserted you, when your accounts are nearing their last few cents or when you are sitting at the bedside of your sick child, that same God who heard the cry of Hagar, who heard the cry of Ishmael, is the same God who is hearing your cry.

Today we will close by writing this verse out in the space below: Psalms 56: 8-11

# HEARING HIS VOICE & WRITTEN IN RED

Week 3 – A Woman At The Well

Day One: Broken, Is Her Name.

"A woman from Samaria came to draw water."

John 4: 7

PRAY ALOUD AND ASK THE LORD TO OPEN YOUR EYES TO THE TRUTH HE HAS WAITING FOR YOU, AND ASK HIM TO TUNE YOUR EARS TO HEAR HIS VOICE.

Bible Reading: John 4: 1 - 30

She accepted who she was. Choices she had made years before continued to cling to her in the form of labels. Her father called her 'shame'. Her mother called her 'disappointment'. Her siblings called her 'embarrassing'. Sometimes men would call her 'beauty', but those moments never lasted.

It was rare that she allowed herself to look deep within and acknowledge the pain, but when she did she knew the choices that led to the labels were only out of a desire to be known, to be loved and to be seen. Each pursuit for love ended miserably. Abandoned. Betrayed. Hurt. Her heart was layered with calluses of self-protection. The fairy tale she dreamed of as a child had long since passed. She now simply looked for provision and maybe if she was lucky, safety.

Keep your head down, so they don't notice you. Eyes to the ground will protect from seeing the crucifying stares and mocking. Do the daily work. Keep him (lover number 5) happy. If he's happy it will be a peaceful day.

Her steps were slow and intentional. Sensible women came to draw water early before the sun rose. She preferred the heat of the day to the scorn of the righteous. Sweat on her brow was welcome above the whispers. It was quiet at the well during mid-day.

Lifting her eyes she immediately saw the man sitting alone at the well. A traveler perhaps? He was a stranger to the village. As she slowly approached she began to see the details of his clothing. He wasn't certainly wasn't a Samaritan and clearly a Jew. The rival of her people. His gazed was fixed on her as she approached, a soft smile as he watched her.

A faint glimmer flickered in her heart. It was so small she nearly missed it, but knew it was there all the same. The fairy tale. The founding fathers of her faith found their brides at the well. Abraham who sent his servant for his son, Isaac and Jacob. At this very well love had come for them. Could today be the day for a fresh start and a new love?

~

John chapter 4 is especially precious to me and this very passage is what caused me to write this Bible study. I relate to her brokenness. The above is what I think happened that day. You see, I can identify with this woman. Perhaps you can too. One seemingly insignificant choice led to another. Choices that seemed insignificant at the time changed the trajectory of the life she had dreamed of as a girl.

Heartache was her familiar friend. Disappointment had become her way of life. Loneliness was the robe she wore daily. When she was a little girl her heart had been full of dreams. The weight of regret was crippling. Each day that pushed further from those dreams helped her accept this place she now resided.

Labels were placed on her as a result of those choices and now she lived one day at a time, having long ago given up on the fairy tale.

The well was indeed a betrothal scene. Stories of Isaac and Jacob would have been passed down from mothers to daughters like we pass down the stories of castles, princesses, and princes coming on a white steed.

I can't help but imagine that she indeed eyed the man sitting at the well with interest. Escape. A glimmer of hope.

Today's lesson will be shorter than lessons we have had in previous days. I'd like today to be a reflection of who she was. Some of us will find we have a lot in common with this woman who had unmet longings. Spend some time reading over chapter 4 of John. Ask the Holy Spirit to reveal to you and open your eyes to see this woman face to face.

List below aspects that you learn about her from your reading:

Hint: verses 7, 9, 15, 17, 18

A woman with 5 husbands in her past, and the man she lived with now was not her husband. We don't know if she had children in or out of wedlock. We know she was the shame of the town, one of the broken women.

She wore labels.

If we are going to truly step into this study we have to resist judging her. This study hit me like a bright yellow school bus when I realized one critical truth: I was her. I wore labels. I made choices. I was broken.

Some of you who are doing this study won't have to stretch far to meet our friend at the well. You're already there, standing with her shoulder to shoulder. You identify, like I do. For others, you may need to look behind you to remember the place from where you came.

Ladies let's all step up to the well and although it may be painful, let's take one step at a time towards vulnerability and approach the well.

What are some labels others have/had for you?

What labels you have placed on yourself?

Do you carry the weight of your past? If so, think about those weights and if you're comfortable list them in bullet points below. This is for your eyes alone.

Can you identify with our new friend? Are you like her and a social outcast? Perhaps you have hid your brokenness, cracks and jagged edges below a cloak of a smile. You know they exist. You do your best to cover them.

We can't judge this woman. Much like the women we studied last week, her unmet and misplaced longings led to choices. Those choices led her further away from her dreams than she ever imagined.

Come to the well vulnerable. When we realize the depth of our need, meeting Him will be so much sweeter. Let's take the masks off.

HEARING HIS VOICE & WRITTEN IN RED

Day Two: Expectations

"The Samaritan woman said to him, "How is it that you, a Jew, ask for a drink from me, a woman of Samaria?" (For Jews have no dealings with Samaritans)."

John 4:9

PRAY ALOUD AND ASK THE LORD TO OPEN YOUR EYES TO THE TRUTH HE HAS WAITING FOR YOU, AND ASK HIM TO TUNE YOUR EARS TO HEAR HIS VOICE.

Bible Reading: John 4: 7 - 11

Today we are going to remove our Levi's, high heels, and hairspray to don the attire of a first century woman. To adequately study the passage and interaction in this portion of Scripture we need to step out of our mindset of the 21st century and acclimate ourselves to the customs and expectations at the scene of the well.

In the article, "Jesus and the women in the gospel of John" Karen Thiessen states the following, which will give us an eyebrow raising glance into the place in society that we would have our feet planted if we lived in the first 1st century:

> *Jewish literature tended to characterize women as unclean, sexual temptresses. The Talmud describes a woman as "a pitcher full of filth with its mouth full of blood, yet all run {54} after her" (Swidler, 3). Since male lust was considered unavoidable due to the seductive nature of women, contact between the sexes was to be avoided. Because women were held responsible for male temptation, they were barred from public life lest they cause a man to sin.*

> *Intellectual initiative on the part of women was not encouraged in Rabbinic Judaism. While study of the Torah was one of man's highest priorities, it was considered a sin for a woman to do the same. Rabbi Eliezer said, "If any man teaches his daughter Torah it is as though he taught her lechery" (Swidler, 93) and, "It is better that the words of the Law be burned, than that they should be given to a woman" (Hurley, 72).*

> *Due to woman's lack of intellectual ability, she was also barred from the role of witness. Josephus states in his Antiquities that "the testimony of women is*

not accepted as valid because of the lightheadedness and brashness of the female sex" (Swidler, 115). (Thiessen, 1990)

Look at John 4: 7. Note who spoke and what was said:

A critical point that will stop us dead in our tracks is this: Jesus came from David's tree but he wasn't considered royalty. At best in those days he was considered a teacher. For those closest to Him (at this time), they knew Him to be the Messiah.

Here is where the cultural significance hits with enough force to knock over every wall still found in Jerusalem:

That he was a man speaking to a woman is shocking.

That He was a rabbi and speaking to a woman, is scandalous.

That He is the Messiah and speaking to a woman, is our invitation.

Jesus was the initiator of the conversation, and as a result He was the Pursuer.

Jot down the critical divide mentioned in verse 9.

Not only do we find that Jesus barged through gender barriers, but He also shook off cultural divides by initiating conversation with this woman, a Samaritan.

Think of your local high school or college football team. It's likely you can name the rivalry faster than you can call out the name of your first dog.

I'm mindful that I'm writing to you ladies whose interest in football may be limited. Allow me this brief analogy. I was born and raised in a small town located in northeast Ohio called Massillon. Football coach and legend, Paul Brown started his career as the head coach for the local high school, the Massillon Tigers. In fact, even to this day, if a male child is born in the local hospital, he is gifted a tiny orange football for his crib.

I am a daddy's girl. From my earliest memories I can recall my dad taking me to his alma mater on a Friday night to watch the games. From the time I was a small girl, driving through the streets in early November, it wasn't uncommon to see stuffed animals of the rival's mascot hanging by a noose in front lawns of the locals. Harsh? Yep it sure is. Likely unacceptable in today's world but in the 1990's it was all fair game. An expressive form of disgust for the rival team. Furthermore, this rivalry was encouraged and fostered in our home. Although I never attended the high school that rivalry was ingrained in me partially as a passion to please my father.

This is the closest illustration that I can come up with that might translate into our culture to understand the tension and division between Jews and Samaritans.

The Samaritans were a group of people that lived in the valley just below Mt. Gerzim. They didn't acknowledge the writings of the Prophets (which included the histories and books such as 1 & 2 Samuel, 1 & 2 Kings, 1 & 2 Chronicles) and the books of wisdom (Psalms, Prov. Etc). These books all placed emphasis on Judea and David's line centered on Jerusalem being the place where the temple of the Living God was to be established. For the Samaritans their traditions stemmed down deep into the history of Abraham, Issac and Jacob exclusively honoring the Pentateuch (Genesis - Deuteronomy).

For the Samaritans, they acknowledged themselves as the true descendants of Abraham and children of the Promise.

Look up the following verses and record your findings below of the location and what took place there:

Deut. 11:29

Deut. 27:12

Joshua 8:33

Samaritans held to the tradition that Schechem, located just below Mt. Gerzim was the location where Abraham built an altar. That same mountain was also the destination of the Israelites when they entered Canaan under Joshua's command. Division between the Jews and Samaritans wasn't improved when in 128 B.C. the Jews invaded and destroyed the temple that the Samaritans had established.

In order to fully put our feet in the shoes of our new friend the Samaritan, let's follow the history of where we stand next to her and the dirt at our feet. Record the place and event that follows:

Genesis 12 : 6 - 7

Genesis 33 : 20

Joshua 24:32

John 4:5

From my research one commentary describes this scene this way:

> *"Jesus broke through two levels of prejudice. The person with whom he spoke was not only a Samaritan but a woman. For a Jewish man to speak to a Samaritan woman was unheard of, and she probably had never experienced a similar conversation. She represents an oppressed minority, still a common reality in much Middle Eastern culture. But Jesus was neither racist nor sexist. He knew that his question would lead to far more than an exchange of words and water."* (Gangel, Holman New Testament Commentary - John, 2000)

In her article mentioned above Thiessen states:

> *"Jewish society frowned upon conversation between male and female. This was particularly true of Samaritan women, who were deemed perpetually unclean. The laws of purity declared that "the daughters of the Samaritans are menstruating {55} from their cradle (Daube, 137). The Samaritan woman's surprised reaction to being addressed by Jesus is evident (4:9). The latter part of the verse is often translated "for Jews have no dealing with Samaritans" (RSV).*
>
> *Jews held to the belief that when a woman was menstruating she was unclean and once her cycle had ended, she needed to go to the temple to be purified. The fact that the Samaritan women were "deemed perpetually unclean" essentially means she wears the first century shame of her cycle, every day of her life.*
>
> *The verb 'sugchrontai' alludes to the cultic code that forbade a Jew to eat or drink from the vessel of an unclean person such as a Samaritan, and especially a Samaritan woman whom they considered a perpetual menstruate. The Samaritan woman's shock is understandable as Jesus requests a drink from her vessel".*

Our precious Jesus, waits for her at the well. A woman. A Samaritan. A women labeled by outsiders as "perpetually unclean" and by those in her town as scandalous.

Hear me clearly sisters, the shame of your past or your present doesn't make you detestable to

Christ. Your heart has always been and will always be desired by Him. The only thing (let me repeat that with emphasis) THE ONLY THING that can keep you from His gaze, His conversation, His arms and His heart is your misconception that you have to come to him in robes rather than rags.

Let that sink in. He knows no limits to where He will go or how far He will extend His hand to reach you where you are as you read this. Nothing you have ever done, nothing that has ever happened to you could ever deter Him from waiting for you at the well. Not only does He sit there waiting, He initiates conversation with you.

Today's Reflections: Spend the day thinking about the Prince who waits for you at the well, rags and all.

Day Three: Quenching Thirst

"If you knew the gift of God, and who it is that is saying to you, 'Give me a drink', you would have asked him, and he would have given you living water."

John 4:9

PRAY ALOUD AND ASK THE LORD TO OPEN YOUR EYES TO THE TRUTH HE HAS WAITING FOR YOU, AND ASK HIM TO TUNE YOUR EARS TO HEAR HIS VOICE.

Bible Reading: Jeremiah 2: 1 - 3, 12 - 13

Do you enjoy camping? I know I do. I don't mind being zipped up in a bag and staring up at the starry night sky. It sounds wonderful doesn't it? The peace of the evening and the animals settling in around you with their evening chorus.

Dawn breaks and reality sets in. The sun rises, the earth comes alive, and you have no running water. I'm not talking about KOA camping. I'm talking about the kind where you hike in and out. Where the starry night of the previous evening doesn't compete with the luxuries of camper lights and electricity.

Are you stuck on the first sentence about no running water? What was your first thought? Having no toilets or having to carry in drinking water and being careful of how much you consumed so it lasts? Remember to use just a little while you brush your teeth and splash water on your face. A shower? That will have to wait.

A remote camping trip is the closest thing we will come to relating with our friend who is sitting at the well with Jesus. That is, unless we travel to a third world country for a missions trip. Even then, for our stay we'll likely have running water. For many of us, we've never lived a life where we can't have immediate access to water by the flip of a lever.

Think back to a time in your life that you would have walked away from Jesus, the fountain of living water, for broken cisterns that can't hold liquid. When I sit and reflect I can distinctly remember what it looked like to live in a constant state of drained and empty.

Jesus looked into the eyes of the woman as He spoke these words:

> *"If you knew the gift of God, and who it is that is saying to you, 'Give me a drink', you would have asked him, and he would have given you living water"*

There's no doubt she was considering her immediate need. As we previously studied, we know she went out at the heat of the day to avoid the whispers and scorn of the other women. When Jesus talks to her about 'living water', there's no doubt she is thinking about a river that must be located near the town that everyone is unaware of.

Can you imagine how luxurious it would be to have flowing water, coming from a stream to bathe in, gather water, and if it was a quiet place folks didn't know about, perhaps some peace while listening to the water trickle.

The key difference to note was that our friend was drawing water from a well that had been dug. This was her access to water for household use, drinking, and personal bathing. In her mind, Jesus was speaking about a luxury that few enjoyed.

One commonality we have with our friend at the well is that although we don't long for the basic necessity of water, we are not left without longings. More than a longing, something we think we can't live without.

Write below a few of your longings:

Now dig deeper. Perhaps this longing is tucked into your past, or something you hold with clenched fists:

I spent the majority of my teens and 20's idolizing romance, fairy tales, a wedding, and a prince. To say I was boy-crazy is an understatement. A stranger could walk into a room and I'd first check for a ring and then consider if he was a fit for what I envisioned my prince would look like. As a result, much like our friend at the well, I lived in a re-occurring cycle of hope and then a broken heart. A desire for a prince and marriage was knit into our hearts so intricately with the finest of threads but when the dream becomes an idol, we are sowing seeds in a ground of desperation with a heart of decay.

Perhaps it's food. Do you turn to food when life gets crazy and the stress is mounting?

Perhaps it's money. Does the mall or amazon call your name when you need a distraction?

Perhaps its attention. Do you turn to someone who is available (romantic or non- romantic) because you're lonely?

Perhaps it's _____

Note the one thing all of the above has in common: The missing element you long for is tangible and most of the time immediate.

Dig Deeper: What is your 'go to' when you need to satisfy a longing?

THERE'S A GOOD CHANCE THE THING YOU LOOK TO FILL YOU, SPEAKS TO THE NAME OF THE EMPTY PLACE.

Just as quick fixes, get rich quick schemes, and promises of immediate satisfactions all leave us disappointed, the one Truth we can hold to is this: Jesus is the One and Only who can and Who *will* fill the empty voids in our lives.

We have a lot vying for our attention. There are empty promises to our left and right claiming the solution to our promise. Personal experience is the one and only way we will be able to understand that Jesus is the only thing that will fill us.

Are you single? Jesus.

Are you craving? Jesus.

Are you struggling with spending? Jesus.

We have to experience Him at night when our arms ache for someone to hold. We have to experience the peace and calming that soothes our souls when we are needy. His beautiful Presence is the only thing that will satisfy our cravings.

Whatever the empty places in your life that you are working to fill, Jesus is the only One who can fill it. In week 5 we will find ourselves at the well with Jesus and we'll look at practical applications about how we can fill those places of longings.

> *"On the last day of the feast, the great day, Jesus stood up and cried out, "If anyone thirsts, let him come to me and drink. Whoever believes in me, as the Scripture has said, 'Out of his heart will flow rivers of living water.'" Now this he said about the Spirit, whom those who believed in him were to receive, for as yet the spirit had not been given, because Jesus was not yet glorified." John 7: 38-39*

Finish off today by reading Isaiah 58. I want you to first pray and ask the Lord to speak to you. Pull out your red pen, and get ready to record below what you feel the Lord is saying to you.

HEARING HIS VOICE & WRITTEN IN RED

Day Four: Leaving It Behind

" So the woman left her water jar..." John 4:28

PRAY ALOUD AND ASK THE LORD TO OPEN YOUR EYES TO THE TRUTH HE HAS WAITING FOR YOU, AND ASK HIM TO TUNE YOUR EARS TO HEAR HIS VOICE.

Bible Reading: John 4: 27-30

She came to the well at noon to avoid scorn and ridicule. Instead a divine appointment had been scheduled without her knowledge. She arrived at a time appointed by God for an encounter. She came with an empty jar and after the experience with Jesus, she left the well so overflowing that she had to share it with the people she had run from and avoided.

I recall reading the book *Heaven's For Real*. It's the story about a little boy who claims to have gone to heaven and come back and recounts the stories of what he saw. In the closing of the book a story is shared of a young girl who has a gift of painting. She sees Jesus in a vision and paints him. A world away, the boy sees that painting and recognizes it as the Man he saw in heaven. It's a story I want to believe.

We often hear amazing stories of healing, divine encounters and miraculous interventions that ignite our hearts and inspire our faith. Although these stories are edifying when we hear them, they don't have life changing powers in and of themselves.

A pastor once wrote that he had a woman in his church who was miraculously healed of disease. The doctors all agreed that the only explanation was being touched by the God, the great Healer. Her family rejoiced and the week following this event, her family joined her in church. They sat next to her for the second, third, and fourth Sundays following her healing. One Sunday weeks later she sat alone with her husband.

The problem with fire is that it burns out unless fueled.

A girl sat in her closet with the lights off. Holding her blanket and pillow she laid on the floor in her desperation. In a land of sin, far away from the place she had left Him, she hoped He could hear her from the distance she had put between them. She cried out to Him and hoped against hope that He would hear her.

He heard her.

She had theological training about the principles and teaching of Jesus, but they were engraved into her mind and had never reached the place that matters: her heart. In that moment in the dark closest something sparked. It was not a fire. Far from it. It was a single spark and in the months that followed she had a personal experience that didn't involve an organized church or Bible doctrine.

She learned that the Holy Spirit is alive and very much a gentleman. With His gentle hand at her back, He found her in that far off land of sin, and gently guided her home. Never pushing, always gentle. Together, hand in hand they returned home.

Ten years later that same girl is not living in the darkness of depression and a closet of defeat. She was forever changed because He found her, touched her, guided her, romanced her, and showed her the way home with Him was through experience.

That same girl is writing this study.

Please hear me on this: It was never intended that we would strictly learn about God and never experience Him. Without a personal experience and a divine encounter, our pursuit for divine intimacy and holiness will fail miserable. We live in a world with arrows being shot at us on a daily basis and land mines placed strategically in our path with the hope that we'll be obliterated. Walking alone with religion is like skipping through a war zone with a bright red umbrella.

A personal experience walking with Jesus doesn't eliminate the war. It elevates the heat of the battle. The primary difference is that our Hero walks into the middle of the battle with bullets flying and shields us with His own body.

Perhaps you can identify with what I've just shared. Perhaps your story is similar, you grew up in church and you know the customs of the organization. Do you find that you sit in the pew aching for more? Do you sense there is something just beyond your grasp but elusive? Sweet one, that unmet desire was placed in your heart so that you would crave and feel your way toward Him.

Don't live a life satisfied with the stories of Jesus other people have shared. Jealously desire a personal encounter with Him at the well. A pursuit by the One who created Romance will always leave you craving more from Him. His pursuit always results in intimate relationship.

Write the following passage of Scripture below: Isaiah 58: 8 - 9

"And the Lord will guide you continually and satisfy your desire in scorched places and make your bones strong; and you shall be like a watered garden, like a spring of water, whose waters do not fail. And your ancient ruins shall be rebuilt; you shall rise up the foundations of many generations; you shall be called the repairer of the breach, the restorer of streets to dwell in."

Isaiah 58: 11 - 12

Read Mark 10:17-23 and write down the differences between the rich young man and our friend at the well.

Him:

Her (John 4:9):

Read Luke 7: 36 - 50 and write down your observations about the encounter:

What would have been the state of her heart to cause her to cry?

To wet His feet with her tears and kiss his feet, what would have been her posture?

What does the Bible imply in verse 39 when it says "If this man were a prophet, he would have known who and what sort of woman this is touching his feet"?

Write verse 47 below:

> Notice verse 49: *"Then those who were at table with him began to say among themselves, "Who is this, who even forgives sins?". We can read this passage and replace the word Pharisees (verses 36, 37, 39) with 'The Religious'. The Pharisees were a group of people who prided themselves on holding to the letter of the law and holding everyone else accountable to the letter of the law. There was no need for a Holy Spirit who convicts, because the Pharisees were on task judging everyone around them over what they were and were not doing. I'm sorry to say that at varying level of extremes we can find Pharisees in today's church.*

I find it ironic that this beautiful act of love by the broken woman was completely missed by the religious in the room. Jesus highlights her actions through teaching a group of judgmental religious folks about what is important and not important in life. Their statement in verse 49 emphasizes the veil that's over their eyes. Their religion doesn't allow them to see the personality of Jesus: Tender, forgiving, and gentle.

Girls, God is passionate about women who are broken. His heart is so tender towards women who come to Him when everyone else has forsaken them. He knows something about being forsaken. He experienced it on the cross when His own Father had to turn His back on the sin He carried *for us*.

Let's return to Jesus sitting at the well. While our friend is running towards town, can't you imagine Jesus sitting at the edge of the well with a grin on His face? Maybe he glasses at the woman's jar sitting at His feet.

Perhaps just perhaps having left that jar means this:

- That jar once represented her former life and she left it at His feet.

- She left it as an offering or sacrifice to Jesus so He could use it.

- She left it so the weight of carrying it wouldn't hinder her from her calling to now share with others.

- In healed by Jesus, she forgot all the things that were once important to her.

Perhaps it's a little of all of the above.

A broken jar can't hold water. But a jar sealed with Jesus not only has the potential to be filled with Holy water, but His Presence always causes our jars to be measured by the overflow. Run sweet sister. As you run, your Living Water within will be shaken and poured out.

Day Five: Transformed, Unafraid, Unashamed

" Come, see a man who told me all that I ever did. Can this be the Christ?"

John 4:29

PRAY ALOUD AND ASK THE LORD TO OPEN YOUR EYES TO THE TRUTH HE HAS WAITING FOR YOU, AND ASK HIM TO TUNE YOUR EARS TO HEAR HIS VOICE.

Bible Reading: John 4: 25-30

I'm a big fan of essential oils. I love that everything we needed, He placed in the garden on the third day. In fact, I was captivated when I heard a doctor state the difference between oils and antibiotics. When we get sick, our cells are literally infiltrated with disease. Antibiotics are designed to wrap around the cells and cover the problem. Have you ever had an antibiotic cover up the symptom, but after you finish taking them, the problem rears up its ugly head again? Me too.

The doctor stated that the difference between antibiotics and essential oils is that the oil has molecules that are so small they can penetrate to the core of a cell within 20 minutes. By penetrating the root of the problem on the inside of the cell, it can clean out each cell and truly heal the problem.

Isn't that so like God? We can try methods, quick fixes, and self helps but none of them will truly penetrate to our core where the problem resides. Only God can do that.

Today we are witnessing that exact event with our friend at the well today.

Read John 4: 25 - 30.

We worship the God who breathed and life began. He's the imagination behind the crystal blue skies and dazzling stars. He's the artist behind every jagged edge of the mountains, and the deep soothing blue of the waves in the sea.

Let's look at an example of a 'macro' view of God: Read Isaiah 40: 12, 26 and write below what you learn about our macro God.

Now let's look at our 'micro' view of God: Read Isaiah 41: 10, 43: 1, 4. This time when you record what you find, I want you to make it personal about yourself. I'll get you started:

_____ does not need to fear, because God is with her (vs 10).

Nothing can be harder to understand or wrap our minds around than a God who formed each and every star, is the same God who looks at you with longing and tenderness. When that very reality penetrates your core and inhabits your cells, get ready for your world to be rocked.

> ROMANS 12:2 SAYS THIS: "DO NOT BE CONFORMED TO THIS WORLD, BUT BE TRANSFORMED BY THE RENEWAL OF YOUR MIND, THAT BY TESTING YOU MAY DISCERN WHAT IS THE WILL OF GOD, WHAT IS GOOD AND ACCEPTABLE AND PERFECT".

The word used in this verse for 'transform' is 'metamorphoo'.

What word comes to mind when you see the transliteration of the above word:

_____

Here's the definition of the word:

> To "change after being with".
>
> "Changing form in keeping with inner reality"

LOOK AGAIN: "TRANSFORMED AFTER BEING WITH"

After being with Jesus and moments of quiet conversation, and after having our hearts touched by Him, we will always, *always* be transformed into being more like him.

We all do crazy, ridiculous, stupid things in our youth. Growing up in a Christian home my whole life, you would think that I would have been on the straight and narrow. However, my deprived heart, dug itself a deep dark pit and my feet jumped into the darkness before I even realized what the end result might be.

Perhaps your path looks similar, or perhaps you have things you'd rather forget. Situations or circumstances that cause you to avoid crowds or push away authentic friendships. We have a desperate desire at our core to be known, but being known requires for someone to know all of us.

When we come to sit at His feet, and look into His eyes, His shadow is going to inevitably fall on us. Furthermore, He is passionate and desires for you to be His. He craves dialogue and conversations with you. He wants you to think about Him, like He thinks and talks about you. And when you look into the reflection of yourself in His eyes, you're not going to see the mistakes in your past, you're going to see His daughter and His bride.

Read the following verses and make them personal to you by owning the verse.

Isaiah 43:10

"I am the Lord's witness......

Isaiah 44:22

A true encounter with Jesus will always leave us changed. The Holy Spirit is the same Person who raised Christ from the dead *(Romans 6:10-11)*. He is the same Person who comes and lives inside you when you take the hand of Jesus and become His.

A truth I have learned though experience is this: The Holy Spirit is 100% a gentleman. He never pushes you, He never tricks you, and He never gives you more than you can handle.

Do you remember meeting your first love? I'm going to take a wild shot in the dark that you did not know everything about him on the first date. I'm also going to take a wild shot in the dark and guess that after a period of time that included long conversations, sharing of thoughts and ideas, experiences together and dates that you came to truly love that person. The same is true of your relationship with Jesus. Intimacy with Him grows through time spent together, talking, and when you simply love on Him in worship.

We all desire to be truly known by Someone.

We all desire to be truly loved by Someone.

We all desire to have a purpose.

Our friend at the well found her desires, when she locked eyes with her destiny. She found her purpose when she experienced His Presence. Her experience led her to immediate action.

We can talk a lot. We can plan a lot. We can even chart out a 3-step process and how to. But until our first step is made, you only have contemplation. We know that our friend at the well had a life changing moment looking into the eyes of the One who knew her when she dropped everything she was doing, left her water jar, and ran into town as fast as her sandal clad feet would take her. She had to share it.

Don't overlook the beauty of this moment. Here's a perfect example of what Jesus can and will do for you.

Show up. Bring Him your brokenness, allow Him to penetrate your heart and then walk away changed.

It's amazing to watch her story unfold and her life be transformed. The people she once tried to avoid, she was now running to. The sin she was trying desperately to hide, she was now freely acknowledging to the entire town. Girls, this didn't take weeks of repeated therapy, this took a single conversation looking straight into the eyes of Jesus for radical transformation to take place. A deep long look into the eyes of Him who formed you, and who loves you no matter where you are, or who you've become will always, always penetrate your core and evoke change.

If you are looking for purpose, and you currently find yourself wondering what you were meant to do, or who you were meant to be, you don't have to look very hard. You were formed in your mother's womb (Psalms 139:13) by a God who loves details. Your personality was shaped, so that your silly jokes, and quirks would be what makes Him smile. Life was breathed into your lungs and from the first moment you cried, He had a plan for you.

You were born to shine. You were born to spend time with Him. You were born to fall deeply in love with Him.

He's the only thing that matters. Let me say that again: He's the only thing that matters.

Get rich quick schemes, beauty supplies, finding Mr. Right, or the smaller dress size is not going to fill that hole. He will fill the hole, and when you begin living out who you were called to be, He will shine through you so that His Presence in your life becomes obvious to everyone around you. At that moment, your pit has been filled with Life giving Water, and you'll overflow.

Week 4 - Refreshing Of The Lord

Day One: Breaking Through And Beyond Barriers

"AND HE HAD TO PASS THROUGH SAMARIA."

John 4:4

PRAY ALOUD AND ASK THE LORD TO OPEN YOUR EYES TO THE TRUTH HE HAS WAITING FOR YOU, AND ASK HIM TO TUNE YOUR EARS TO HEAR HIS VOICE.

Bible Reading: John 4: 1-4

In our third week of study we put our toes into the shoes of brokenness, and together we were with her as we sat down with Jesus and looked into the transformation power of the Savior.

We were never meant to come to the well with our brokenness and leave the same way. Just like the woman at the well, she chose to sit in Light, not run from it. She chose to run with Light to those she once tried to avoid. That alone is the transformation power of Someone who heals, binds up, and romances our heart.

This week in our study we are going to step next to Jesus and look at this encounter from His perspective.

Our key verse for today is John 4:4 and it's a short one.

"And He had to pass through Samaria."

Let's grab our shovels and dig up this treasure together. It's been planted there for you and this specific moment. Many people may walk on the soil of God's Word, but for those with the metal detector (the Spirit) and who are willing to dig, there are treasures that will literally change your entire world. To grasp the full meaning of this verse, we need to look at the original text.

A LITERAL TRANSLATION OF THIS VERSE IS:

"MOREOVER IT WAS NECESSARY FOR HIM TO PASS THROUGH SAMARIA".

Let's dig a little further. The Greek word for "necessary" is 'dei' and it means:

"what is absolutely necessary, what must happen".

Now let's look at another verse in the Bible that uses that same exact word.

Turn to Luke chapter 2 and read verses 41 - 52.

Here we find Jesus as a 12-year-old boy who during his yearly trip to Jerusalem to celebrate Passover, strays from the watchful eyes of His parents and makes His way to the Temple. I mean, where else would He go?

List below the things that jump out at you or strike you in this passage:

His poor, heartsick mother must have been sick with worry for three days straight thinking that she lost the Promised Child. While she was sick with worry, "He was sitting among teachers, listening to them and asking them questions". I love verse 47. **Write it below:**

Back to the lesson. Did you catch where the word the "must needs go", or "necessary" is?

Don't feel discouraged if you didn't. The word is actually translated differently and it will be eye opening. Here's a hint. Look at verse 49.

*"Why were you looking for me? Did you not know that I **must be** in my Father's house?"*

Who is it in your life that you submit to their direction?

You likely mentioned a husband, employer, parent, church leader, government official or all the above. There's only one person to whom Jesus would submit to: His Father, The Most Holy God.

Let's now go back to our passage in John 4:4. It wouldn't be a stretch to say that we can paraphrase the verse like this:

> BECAUSE OF HIS FATHER'S DESIRE AND COMMAND, HE HAD TO PASS THROUGH SAMARIA. HE WAS COMPELLED TO GO.

Expositors commentary says this:

> "The shortest route from Jerusalem to Galilee lay on the high road straight through Samaritan territory. Many Jews would not travel by that road, for they regarded any contact with Samaritans as defiling"

Its not just that the route He took was the less fashionable path and it wasn't even that He strode through the "bad part of town". He went there and sat down at a place that all of his friends, and the people in his upbringing would think was defiling. And by defiling I mean literally to be made unclean. The Jews took extraordinary measures (and still do today) to hold to the very line of each letter of the law. To willingly walk and sit down near a place and people who could make you unclean was nothing short of scandalous.

I love this quote by Expositors:

> "It meant leaving the usually traveled highway that was well known and comfortable. It meant traveling without the usual companions. And when Jesus went into Samaria as an outsider, risk was joined to cost. As any traveler knows, prices change when the retailer hears your accent."

Why was He compelled to go? There were decades of combat, attacks, rivalries and fighting between the Jews in Jerusalem and the Samaritans. We saw that last week. He was compelled to go because He and the Father knew that (as we will come to see later this week) that there were people there who were ready to meet and receive Jesus.

I also think there's another reason. A reason that's closely knit into Jesus's heart.

He went out of His way and broke through every social barrier for one woman.

For. One. Broken. Woman.

Just let that sit with you for a minute. All that distance and all those raised eyebrows, because a heart was broken, lonely and had likely given up hope of a fairy tale. Jesus being the Prince He is, sat at a well and waited for her.

HEARING HIS VOICE & WRITTEN IN RED

Day Two: His Refreshing

"...I have food to eat that you do not know about."

John 4:32

PRAY ALOUD AND ASK THE LORD TO OPEN YOUR EYES TO THE TRUTH HE HAS WAITING FOR YOU, AND ASK HIM TO TUNE YOUR EARS TO HEAR HIS VOICE.

Bible Reading: John 3: 1 - 21

It was 3:00 in the afternoon and from my home office, I gazed with longing to my overstuffed chair and blanket. There was a constant battle of pings from both my phone and my laptop. Deadlines, demands, to do lists left undone and overwhelm flooding my soul. I'm writing with confidence that you can relate to this scenario that regularly occurs. Whether it's tasks pulling at you or children at your feet, the demands of life seem to be at an all-time high next to our extreme accessibility and the demands for our immediate response.

Although Jesus didn't experience social media (did He intentionally pick ancient Jerusalem because it was pre-social media?), He did know what it was to have throngs of people begging, grasping, and reaching for his attention. Jesus knew a thing or two about demands. He was also intimately aware of what it meant to be worn out.

Aren't you thankful we have a Prince at the well who personally has experienced and knows full well what it means to be stretched thin, pulled tight and flat worn out?

Let's start today by looking at John 4 as a whole.

Compare verses 1 - 6 with verses 31 - 34.

Note your comparisons and jot down what you notice:

Now, let's look back at yesterday and note below the one thing that stood out most to you and spoke to you (remember to look for what you wrote in red):

For me personally I sat in complete awe for days while writing day one and day two this week. I couldn't stop thinking about the Prince who not only deliberately went out of His way for a broken woman, but who stared down scorn, disgust and judgment in its face and pursued this woman.

Today we'll see Jesus in a different light. He's coming to us today weary and we're going to see how he finds rejuvenation. Let's dive into this truth and see what we can uncover.

Today we'll start in Scripture by looking back at today's Bible reading, John chapter 3 verses 1 - 21.

If you haven't already read today's Bible reading, go ahead and do so now.

Note your observations and comparisons between our friend at the well and Nicodemus.

Continuing with your thoughts above, I have a couple listed below to help you further your comparison. Compare the following:

Social Status:

Religious Training:

Lifestyle:

Time Of Day:

Very good! You dug in hard and are taking what we've learned about our friend at the well, and are digging in deep to compare our broken friend to a leader in the religious realm of influence.

Write below your personal takeaway and insight from this work you've done:

For religious training, we see that he was trained up in the best schools and with the best teachers money could afford. He would know his history and his religion backwards, forwards and be a cross referencing genius. Our friend on the other hand, would never have been taught and likely couldn't read. Her knowledge only came from hearing what her family told her or what she may have been taught at religious gatherings where she would have been segregated with the other women.

Verse 2 of chapter 3 is insightful when we first learn that this Pharisee named Nicodemus (a ruler/leader of the Jews) is coming to Jesus by night. We've already learned that our dear friend (to avoid scorn) came in the light of day at high noon. The commonality we can draw between these two people is that both likely spoke with Jesus at a time when they were trying to avoid the prying eyes of onlookers. However, the primary difference between Nicodemus and our friend at the well is that our friend was trying to avoid scorn and not seeking Jesus.

Jesus found *her*.

Nicodemus, cloaked in the cover of darkness "came to Jesus" with intention.

Nicodemus came under the cover of night to avoid the onlookers because he feared the judgment of being seen talking to Jesus. Our sweet bit of brokenness at the well was avoiding onlookers because of her own shame, but openly sat in the broad light of day while Jesus probed into her life and uncovered her shame.

In John's gospel, he refers to light and darkness on numerous occasions that we know there's theological depth to these words.

Let's look at some of those examples and write down what you observe from these verses about light and darkness:

John 1: 6 - 9

John 3:19- 21

John 8: 12

John 9: 4 - 5

One of the primary differences between Nicodemus and the woman at the well is response to their conversations with Jesus.

Note the response of Nicodemus and subsequent action (if any):

Note the response of the Samaritan woman:

One commentator said it best this way:

> "As Nicodemus's character fell silent in chapter 3, leaving us to wonder what would become of this religious Jewish leader, suddenly we see that this irreligious woman takes the unexpected step:
>
> She acknowledges Jesus' lordship, remains "in the light", and exhibits some of the signs of discipleship. She runs and tells others, bringing them to Jesus, and as a result many come to believe". (Burge, 2000)

Today we've established the primary difference between Jesus's conversation with a religious leader and his conversation with an outcast.

Let's go back where we started and look at Jesus's response. Refer to your notes from the start of our day and recap Jesus's response that we already discussed. What is your takeaway from this?

These two verses (John 4:6 and John 4:31) couldn't speak louder if they had am amplifier connected to them. We can see Jesus coming to the well weary and likely hungry (the reason the disciples went in search of food) and after his conversation with the Samaritan woman, He is refreshed and revived.

His disciples bring back food, see him speaking to a woman (insert shock here) and ask him to eat.

"Rabbi eat". He turns, looks at them, and says "I have food to eat that you do not know about.....my food is to do the will of him who sent me to accomplish his work".

It's not clear in the text what exactly revived Jesus and caused Him to be refreshed with renewed energy, so we can look at the dialogue as a whole to draw our own conclusions.

My personal summary is that when he approached this woman who is cast off by everyone else, finds she is willing to have open dialogue with Him and as He draws her out into conversation, slowly reveals Himself to her, in short I think He is revived by her response to Him.

She came in bright sunlight: He is the Light.

She had been called names: He was the One who calls by name.

She was desperate: He was desperate for her.

He spoke: She responded

He asked: She sassed

He taught: She questioned

He probed: She deflected

He pursued: She stayed

He revealed: She was His

# HEARING HIS VOICE & WRITTEN IN RED

Day Three: The Divine Pursuit

"Go call your husband, and come here."

John 4:16

PRAY ALOUD AND ASK THE LORD TO OPEN YOUR EYES TO THE TRUTH HE HAS WAITING FOR YOU, AND ASK HIM TO TUNE YOUR EARS TO HEAR HIS VOICE.

Bible Reading: John 4:10

In week 1 and 2 we established that the well was a betrothal scene. Although it's not written into the text, a woman's heart and her innate longings, dreams and wishes don't change much over time. Scripture states that the man she was living with now wasn't her husband (John 3: 18). She no doubt had spent most of her life living with unmet longings and now after having been married 5 times, she was living with the next guy who had come along. Unmet longings are tattooed to this woman's story.

The one thing that is true is that unmet longings transition us into becoming opportunist.

I spent most of my life (prior to my marriage) being a marriage opportunist. I didn't need to know a guy for more than 5 minutes, before I started contemplating if he was "the one". Ok, let's be honest here. I didn't even need to speak a word to a man before I started wondering if he was "the one".

Praise you Jesus, for rescuing this broken woman. In fact, before any one of us sit here in the 21st century and judge this sweet lady for having 5 husbands, I am going to draw the line in the sand and step over to where she is. Far be it from me, to think that I am any different from her when no sin is greater in the eyes of God than another. In fact, my past is so tainted with darkness, it may as well have been 5 husbands.

Some of you will be able to relate to her and there's others of you that won't be able to relate. I bless you indeed. But you will have had different sin struggles and so I hope you'll translate this to your personal situation.

The reality of it is that all of us who have lived with unmet longings, subsequent broken hearts, and failed relationships are just waiting for that Prince to come along who will make our dreams come true.

So when our sweet friend approaches that well, don't you think she was thinking "is this Him"? Oh sweet friend, hold on tight because that's what He's after.

Identify who spoke first in this passage and identify which verse it is located in.

Record what was said:

Remember back to day 1 of this week where we identified that walking through Samaria and Jesus's "must needs go" translated into breaking Jewish common practice of avoiding all things defiling (Samaria).

Write out the significance you see with Jesus's question to her:

In the eyes of Jesus's people (Jews), Samaria wasn't just the "other side of the tracks", it was walking into a hospital room filled with infectious diseased people and touching every single surface and then rubbing your tongue with the same hands. It was defiling. When Jesus asks to drink from her cup, He wasn't just asking to touch something she touched. He was asking to drink and touch to His lips the pot she carried daily.

Scandalous Jesus.

With this single action Jesus would have become instantly unclean in the eyes of any observing Jews.

TRUTH:

We don't need to change who we are to sit down and get to know Jesus.

Jesus the Prince of our heart looks past the scars of our past. He looks beyond the smudges of sin, and He sees the heart that carries the weight of longing that He knows only He can release.

Read verse 10.

If she knew what:

He would give what:

Let's look at the word "gift" and do a word study together. If possible, grab your smartphone or computer and go to this website:

Www.biblehub.com

In the search bar at the top, type in John 4:10

Then, I want you to select "Lexicon" in the top bar.

Then go to the word "gift" and click on 1431 next to it.

Here you have the transliteration of that word from Greek to English:

Write below your findings about this word: dōrean

The word *gift* here denotes favor. It is the favor of the Lord to bestow on her something she desperately needs, despite not having done anything at all to deserve it.

The Lord is speaking in an allegory about what He wants to give her. Yet in her humanity, she (like the disciples) couldn't see past the physical to comprehend the meaning or understand the full magnitude of what He was actually saying.

One thing we should be mindful of is that often times we need to minister to the physical needs of those we come in contact with before we can minister to the spiritual needs. For a person who is starving or cold, it's very difficult to think past their immediate physical need to get to the spiritual.

Here our friend needs divine revelation by the One who is speaking to her. He has to penetrate the darkness that cloaks her, so she can have a glimpse of what He's saying.

John Calvin described it this way:

> "He compared human reason to a man walking through a field in the dark of night. We are like travelers 'who in a momentary lightning flash see far and wide, but the sight vanishes so swiftly that (they are) plunged again into the darkness of the night before (they) can even take a step'. God illumines us sufficiently for us to know that there are villages and mountains on the horizon, but we cannot make a map or find our way successfully. Spiritual transformation is thus an act of grace that enables us to understand the things we yearn to know."

Having a firm knowledge (like Nicodemus) of Bible doctrine is one thing, but it won't penetrate the heart until there is a personal experience where a person is touched by the One who causes eyes to see.

> *"The woman answered him, 'I have no husband'. Jesus said to her, 'You are right in saying, 'I have no husband; for you have had five husbands, and the one you have now is not your husband. What you have said is true".*

Notice that in our reading, the walls of her heart don't come down until Jesus speaks a word of prophesy over her and calls out what only she would know. Certainly a stranger who isn't from the town (verse 19) couldn't know these things. By this Word over her life and His revealing of being the one who knows her intimately, her heart becomes open to who He might be.

The fact that she didn't deny these facts about her lifestyle says something about her. Instead her response was "sir, I perceive you are a prophet". She deflected, but she remained. By remaining in His presence, she's now in a place where Jesus can pour into her open heart.

Let's also look at how Jesus slowly reveals Himself to her:

Jesus walks to the well as a man who needs a drink.

She calls him "_____" (verse 11).

What does she call him in Verse 19: _____

She confesses she knows someone is coming. Who is that (verse 25):

Jesus Response:

Do you see the progression and unfolding as the conversation continues and she comes into deeper awareness and knowledge of who it is she is speaking to?

        Jesus the man

        Prophet

        Messiah

        I Am

        Rabbi (Teacher)

        Savior Of The World

In order to grasp the weight of significance in verse 26 is to first write it out. Go ahead and do that below:

This is the covenant name for God and God alone in the Old Testament. Let's look for ourselves:

Read Exodus 3: 13 – 14. What name did God tell Moses to use to refer to Him:

Use of the words "ego eimi" by Jesus in verse 26 is directly telling this woman that Yahweh, the God of her ancestors, Abraham, Issac and Jacob is the same Person speaking to her now.

Jesus often spoke in parabels or in allegory with his disciples or when asked a question by observers. Instead of allegory Jesus cuts through poetic rhetoric and is more candid than we'll see anywhere else in Scripture. I believe the candidness of the conversation reveals the heart of the Jesus desiring her to know very clearly who He is.

The only other time God ever directly comes out and reveals who He is as the "I AM", is at His trial.

During all the time spent with his disciples, all of his teaching in various places, he never directly comes out and confesses those words again until the day when He goes before the people who will put Him on the cross.

That my friends, should cause us to sit back and realize with deeper understanding the compassionate heart of Jesus who desires broken women to be His.

Today's lesson has taken us straight to the heart of Jesus and shown us that He desires to be known by us. Spend the rest of today's quiet time and throughout the rest of your day dwelling on this truth and allowing what this means by having a Prince who is waiting for you to know Him intimately.

HEARING HIS VOICE & WRITTEN IN RED

Day Four: Worship In Spirit and Truth

"God is spirit, and those who worship him must worship in spirit and truth."

John 4:24

PRAY ALOUD AND ASK THE LORD TO OPEN YOUR EYES TO THE TRUTH HE HAS WAITING FOR YOU, AND ASK HIM TO TUNE YOUR EARS TO HEAR HIS VOICE.

Bible Reading: John 4: 19 - 26

I have spent a significant amount of time photographing in the wild of the Canadian Rockies. During that time I have come to learn two things: The mountains can be a haven of majesty however they can also be a place where the weather changes in a single moment and you can be dangerously caught off guard.

Today our friend is confronted with eyes of love while her sin is called out. Let's look at it again to set our context:

Review John 4: 16 - 18

Notice her subsequent response in verse 19 and jot your observations below:

She acknowledged Him as a prophet and indirectly confirmed His statement by omission. Before He could dig into her heart any deeper, she deflected by moving straight to religious divides.

Religion is one of the most popular barricades to hide behind.

Today we can find many situations in the church and Christian communities where people place greater emphasis on tradition and Christian culture than they do Truth.

Note a few instances you have encountered below:

Let's look at Jesus's response in verse 21:

> *"Jesus said to her, 'Woman, believe me, the hour is coming when neither on this mountain nor in Jerusalem will you worship the Father. You worship what you do not know; we worship what we know, for salvation is from the Jews. But the hour is coming, and is now here, when the true worshipers will worship the Father in spirit and truth, for the Father is seeking such people to worship him."*

Here we see Jesus speak three sentences. Outline the point made in each sentence:

1)

2)

3)

There is a critical moment to this beautiful interaction that can be missed if not carefully dissected.

Jesus in verse 18 called out her sin and in verse 19 she had a choice. She could get up and walk away from the conversation or she could stay and look Truth directly in the eyes.

All He needed was her honesty to be able to move forward. Notice He didn't dissect her life or her past choices. She acknowledged the Truth by calling Him a prophet, and then she hid behind a religious boundary (which mountain should believers worship on).

Jesus isn't going to get hung up on religion, but He does hold to the Truth of the matter with blunt clarity.

Salvation is indeed from the Jews (from Jesus). As we recall from week 1 of our study, the Samaritans long held the belief that Mt. Gerzerim was the place where God met with Moses; A holy place. Jerusalem and the place of King David and Solomon's Temple, were the place the Presence of God had filled the temple and where the believers traveled to worship each Passover.

This was a hot issue for the time and demographic. Imagine modern day charismatic's going toe to toe with conservative Baptists.

Verse 24 and the next statement by Jesus changes everything and drives a spike directly at the heart of the conversation. Here He will unfold and reveal more to this broken woman than He has with anyone to this point. **He makes three statements, summarize them below:**

The time had come, when physical location wouldn't matter, and the location of one's heart would mean everything. The Father was seeking those who would accept this transition away from religious tradition.

Here enters the Holy Spirit. "God is spirit, and those who worship him must worship in spirit and truth".

Look up John 6:35 and record below what Jesus refers to Himself as:

Look up I John 5: 6- 8 and record who is Truth:

Read John 7: 37 - 39 and fill in the blanks:

"On the last day of the feast, the great day, Jesus stood up and cried out, "If anyone _____, let him come to me and drink. Whoever believes in me, as the Scripture has said, 'Out of his heart will flow _____'". Now this he said about the _____, whom those who believed in him were to receive, for as yet the _____ had not been given, because Jesus was not yet glorified".

The Spirit was coming, and the Spirit would change everything. Let's look at what Jesus tells the disciples later in His ministry about the coming of the Spirit.

Read John 16: 4 – 15 and John 14: 25 - 27 and note your observations about the coming of the Spirit, and what He will do below:

Often times I sit in absolute longing to be able to see the face, smile, and eyes of Jesus. When he states in verse 7 "it is to your advantage that I go away..." I am amazed at the realization of what that actually means.

Turn to John 14: 12 - 14 and based on what we just learned about it being to our advantage of Jesus going away, and the Holy Spirit coming, record what He says:

Jesus had gone into a place many pilgrims traveled to worship: The temple (a sacred place). He overturned tables, reprimanded, and wiped clean the trade that was taking place. Radical actions in a respected place.

He then broke all rules, traditions and propriety by speaking with a less than lower class Samaritan who also happened to be likely one of the most scandalous women in town.

If you think for one moment that Jesus cares about propriety, you are reading with biased eyes because there was nothing proper or safe about Jesus.

Sinless: Yes.

Proper: No.

Religion had absolutely no place in the room with Jesus. What religion controlled, Jesus consumed. Strict regulations, rules and codes attempted to control.

Jesus with His outpouring of love, invites us to a better way, a better life, and a better love.

It's much easier to follow someone when you know they are giving direction from a place of passionate love than it is to follow after angry shouts of command.

Laws regulate, shrink, demand and control.

Love allures, guides, invites, draws out, and breathes life.

HEARING HIS VOICE & WRITTEN IN RED

Day Five: Refreshed

"...I have food to eat that you do not know about ."
John 4:34

PRAY ALOUD AND ASK THE LORD TO OPEN YOUR EYES TO THE TRUTH HE HAS WAITING FOR YOU, AND ASK HIM TO TUNE YOUR EARS TO HEAR HIS VOICE.

Bible Reading: Hosea 2: 14 - 16

She received news that shook her to her core. Life would never be the same. While shock passed into that very realization, she needed someone with her that would understand.

Whether it's death, finances, sickness, someone walking out, or someone walking in, it's always an easier road to travel when you can walk alongside that road with someone who knows the path. Someone who has been there before.

I received word that Don suddenly passed away. He was my father's dearest friend while we were missionaries in Canada. My heart instantly broke for his sweet wife Evelyn. Evelyn is a first nations woman who has more skill for creating beautiful moccasins and clothing than anyone I've ever met. Don and Evelyn had been together for as long as I can remember, and now he was gone. Heart breaking, I called a sweet friend who lived next door to us in the small village of Anzac and to my surprise (although it shouldn't have been), Evelyn was with her that very moment. Why? Margaret had lost her husband years before. You cannot understand the heart of a widow until you've walked that road.

If you lose a child, nobody will understand that pain like another parent who knew what it was like to watch their baby draw its last breath.

If you find that your fairy tale ended up striking midnight and the romance is over, nobody will understand like someone whose toes also touched the threshold of divorce court.

If you hear the word 'cancer' coming from your doctor's lips, nobody will understand that journey like the person next to you while you sit in chemo or radiation.

Nobody, except for Jesus.

Please can we put aside our Sunday School Jesus, and recognize that this Man we have been following at the well for the last four weeks is the same One who sits next to you now?

He waited for her at the well. He is waiting for you to look in His direction.

Even more than that, not only does He look deep within you and clearly sees the pain, He understands it more profoundly than you can imagine.

Betrayed? He felt that.

Loss of a beloved friend or family member? He felt that.

Loneliness? He knew it all too well.

My husband doesn't travel through life's difficult moments with me while sitting on the sidelines. He doesn't watch while I go through trials. He's with me in the thick of it. Together we receive the news, together we process it, and together we work through it emotionally. Pain shared, sleepless nights together, and endless conversations.

Look up Hosea 2:16 and write it below:

I distinctly remember being in college when someone that was very important in my life walked out. Under a tree on that Christian University, this verse jumped off the page and straight into my heart with a lightning bolt straight to my soul.

"You will call me 'My Husband'….".

All my young heart longed for was the prince, the wedding and the happily ever after. In that moment under the tree, all hope seemed lost, except for a truth that I could barely wrap my mind around, a truth that a Prince had been waiting under that tree for me and even in that moment was next to me, calling Himself my Husband.

Note the passage doesn't say "You will call me Husband". There's one word that when added means ownership, "My". "You will call me **My** Husband". A husband who walks alongside you, who cries when you cry, who sings songs of love over you, who when you feel waves of peace roll over you, you know it's His caress.

This is why He came, and as I write this on Easter Sunday, this is why He died. Because of women at the well like our friend, because He knew I needed a Husband under that tree, and because He planned for you to have this Bible Study in your hands at this moment in your life, so that you could know too (with certainty) that He is right next to you and wants you to speak these words: "My Husband".

Religion shoves you into the door of uncomfortable and difficult situations.

Relationship enters with you.

Just breathe out his name with me will you? Whisper it. Feel it.
"Jesus. Jesus. Jesus."

Let's look back at Hosea chapter 2 and read verses 14 - 15.

> "Therefore, behold, I will allure her, and bring her into the wilderness, and speak tenderly to her. And there I will give her her vineyards and make the Valley of Achor a door of hope. And there she shall answer as in the days of her youth, as at the time when she came out of the land of Egypt".

If you'll allow me this small liberty, I'd like to personalize what this means in today's day:

THEREFORE, BEHOLD, I WILL ALLURE _____, AND BRING HER INTO THE WILDERNESS, AND SPEAK TENDERLY TO HER. AND THERE I WILL GIVE HER VINEYARDS AND MAKE THE VALLEY OF TROUBLE A DOOR OF HOPE. AND THERE SHE SHALL ANSWER AS IN THE DAYS OF HER YOUTH, AS AT THE TIME WHEN SHE CAME OUT OF BONDAGE AND SLAVERY.

If we can be certain about anything, it's that every fairy tale of the Prince coming to the rescue was written directly about Jesus. Over and over throughout the entirety of the Bible, we can see the Prince coming to the rescue, saving His people. From the flight out of Egypt to the woman who had crowds waiting to stone her.

His heart is that of One who rescues.

What do you need Him to rescue you from now? Write it below:

Have you talked to Him about it? Try talking to Him now as you would speak to your Husband.

A Prince went out of His way, He sat in the heat of the day while she walked towards the well, and then He lovingly and patiently drew her out of her brokenness. He never threw accusations at her. He never used guilt. His loving eyes penetrated deep into her soul. Perhaps this is the reason why when His disciples came back wondering who had given Him food.

Clearly when the disciples had departed for the village for food and had come back with it a short time later, they were truly perplexed over this rejuvenated Jesus.

Looking around, they saw no food. Look at John 4:33 and record what was said below:

"My food is to do the will of Him who sent me and to accomplish His work"
(verse 34).

That was His response. A revitalized Jesus. Once weary (verse 6), and now refreshed.

Why do you think Jesus was refreshed?

Have you found your sweet spot in life? I hope you have. Personally speaking, my sweet spot is when I'm speaking to a group of women, or photographing all alone in the middle of a forest. Those are my sweet spots. Sweet spots are moments in your life where you know you are living out your calling.

What are *your* sweet spots?

Next week we are going to look at how these lessons we have learned are applied practically to our lives, but for now, let's keep our eyes locked on Jesus.

He had found His sweet spot. The broken. The sick. The troubled. The hurting. The hungry. The prisoner. When He poured out Himself, His Words, His touch, He was filling Himself back up. That's what He does today. He pours out His Presence and His Peace, and then He smiles and delights when we realize and receive it.

How would your life change today if you were able to understand with a fresh new clarity that Jesus is much closer than you ever dreamed?

Let's close today with a prayer asking Him for spiritual awareness to His Presence, His smile, His voice and His desires.

HEARING HIS VOICE & WRITTEN IN RED

WEEKLY RECAP

Week 5 – Finding Our Well

Day One: A Purpose Revealed

"I will instruct you and teach you in the way you should go;

I will counsel you with my eye upon you."

Psalms 32:8

PRAY ALOUD AND ASK THE LORD TO OPEN YOUR EYES TO THE TRUTH HE HAS WAITING FOR YOU, AND ASK HIM TO TUNE YOUR EARS TO HEAR HIS VOICE.

Bible Reading: Exodus 2: 1 - 22

Sweet one, we have traveled four weeks together and met women just like us. We started in Genesis and traveled through to the Gospel of John.

Now we'll dig our shovels into the most difficult week as we look at our final woman: You.

I'm going to shoot this to you straight: This can either be an easy week to skim through and finish without difficulty, or it can be the hardest and most life changing week in this study.

I have been praying that this study would find you in a perfect moment that can only be ordained by God. If that's the case, likely paragraphs have already struck chords in your heart by the all-knowing hands of the Spirit. If that's the case, I'm going to ask you to please spend extra time in prayer today asking the Lord to reveal to you truth, purpose, and above all, Himself in this coming week.

Together, I'm going to pick up my walking stick and we will walk this week out. Our wells may look very different, but one thing will tie it all together: The One who is waiting for us to join Him.

Let's find the fairy tale.

Our Bible reading today took us to Exodus 2 where we met Moses. If you didn't take the time to read it, please go back, read it, and meet me back here.

Moses was a man who lived a life with a theme: Escape.
List below two examples of this from your reading:

Moses came from a lineage of the tribe of Levi. They would have been people who believed in the God of Abraham, Isaac and Jacob, just like we studied in week 2. Those stories would have been passed down and shared with passion to their children.

Chapter one of Exodus finds Pharaoh oppressing Israel by asking the midwives to kill the babies who bear a son (Exodus 1:16). When the midwives didn't do as Pharaoh demanded, a command went out to all the people that every Hebrew male son would be thrown into the Nile.

This brings us to the day of Moses's birth, when his mother hides him for 3 months.

Let's pick up at Chapter 2:1.
Answer the following questions:

- What did Moses's mother notice about her child (verse 2)?

- Look up Acts 7:20 and record what is said about Moses by Stephen:

- Now look up 1 Samuel 16:7 and record what you learn about God:

Society in the days of Moses and still today places a great deal of emphasis on outward appearances. Oftentimes our success (or lack thereof) is unfairly hinged on our appearance and whether or not it conforms with expectations. I don't know about you, but I'm thankful that even on my darkest days, God doesn't look at my circumstances, He sees my heart.

Let's look at what Moses's mother did to save him. Record it below (verses 3 - 4).

Record what transpires in your own words (verses 5 - 10).

Why did Pharaoh's daughter call the babe Moses?

Isn't it ironic that the same place where Moses was supposed to see death as a baby, is also the same place he finds redemption?

Why did Moses have to flee Egypt (verse 11 - 14)?

What was Pharaoh's reaction (verse 15)?

Once again Moses finds himself the target of Pharoah's wrath and while man has plans for his death, God has different plans.

Where does Moses go?

I hope by now in our study that when you see a situation at the well in Scriptures that your pulse is quickening and you know life changing Truth is waiting for you.

Before we dive into the scene at the well, let's look at some commonalities. Anytime we can identify similarities in Scripture there is usually a treasure waiting for us. God is a God of intention. Nothing is by chance or a coincidence with Him.

Without looking at your Bible, record the answers to the questions below:

Where were the midwives supposed to put the babies to their death?

Where did Moses's mother place her baby?

Why did Moses receive the name that he did?

When Moses flees Pharaoh a second time, where does he end up?

What is the one thing all the above situations have in common?

Friend, if you wrote the 5 letter word water you are absolutely correct.

In fact, water is an important theme in the first chapters of John that lead up to our friend at the well. Look below and read the stories if you feel lead to do so:

Jesus is baptized with water: John 1: 29 - 34

Jesus turns water into wine: John 2: 1 - 12

Jesus speaks to Nicodemus about rebirth, "unless one is born of water and the Spirit he cannot enter the kingdom of God": John 3: 1 -8

Let's turn back to Exodus and look at chapter 2, verse 16. Moses has arrived at Midian and the priest there has 7 daughters. As I'm sure they did on a daily basis, they brought their sheep to the well to draw water for them. On this particular day we find that they are chased away by the shepherds.

Do you remember why Moses had to flee Egypt? He saw an Egyptian beating one of the Hebrews: his people. Now after fleeing Egypt and literally running for his life, you would think he would learn his lesson. Clearly our friend Moses has something etched into his being that calls him out to save the persecuted.

Could it be that when Moses's mother looked at him and saw a "fine child" (ESV), that she was prompted by God to see the valiant heart of a warrior who would redeem the chosen people from the hands of Egypt?

Here at the well not only do we find Moses being the rescuer, but he literally "stood up, and saved them, and watered their flock" for them.

As with our stories from week 2, record what takes place as a result of this scene (verse 21):

Today we learned that redemption was found for Moses in the water. Even at birth His mother noticed something different about him. Often times we think Moses must have been the firstborn, but in actuality he already had siblings. His mother had a gut instinct that somehow this child was destined with a calling.

I so much wish that we could sit across from each other and you could tell me about your childhood. My prayer is that you had people in your life who at a young age spoke life and blessings over you. If you didn't, right now in this moment, I want to speak truth over your life.

WHEN OTHERS HAVE DEFINED YOU, RANKED YOU, STACKED YOU, AND DICTATED OUTCOMES FOR YOU, GOD SAW DEEP INTO YOUR HEART AND HAS DECLARED PURPOSE FOR YOU. YOU ARE SUPPOSED TO BE WALKING WITH CONFIDENCE IN YOUR STEP, WALKING LIKE A WARRIOR PRINCESS.

I want you to take a couple moments to analyze your life so far, and answer the following questions:

Like Moses, what is one thing you were physically saved from in your childhood or adolescent life:

Summarize the scenario above with one word:

_____

For Moses, he found longings in his heart that brought out action. For him, it was the heart of a rescuer. Yours may look very different, but can you analyze your heart right now and identify a topic, issue or theme you are particularly passionate about?

_____

Amy Carmichael, an early missionary said this:

"It's a safe thing to trust Him to fulfill the desires He creates".
_____

If there is one thing the enemy doesn't want, it's people who are defined by awareness over who they were intended to be in Christ. So if you're struggling to identify your theme, don't give up. Take it to God in prayer and ask him to reveal to you the theme of your life.

If however you were able to identify the thing that stirs your heart up, what would life look like if you walked in confidence knowing that you had a holy purpose, a holy calling, and a holy success just waiting for you to walk through?

It's God honoring to dream big dreams, if they are rooted in a passionate heart for His will.

Today, I hope your heart is awaking to the God sized dreams that He has planted in your life. Maybe they've laid dormant for a season, or perhaps you hadn't realized they were planted to begin with but now you're starting to see sprouts of hope. Let today be the day you validate those longings by writing them in red below with Jesus.

HEARING HIS VOICE & WRITTEN IN RED

Day Two: Divine Intimacy

"And they heard the sound of the Lord God walking in the garden in the cool of the day…"

Gen 3:8

PRAY ALOUD AND ASK THE LORD TO OPEN YOUR EYES TO THE TRUTH HE HAS WAITING FOR YOU, AND ASK HIM TO TUNE YOUR EARS TO HEAR HIS VOICE.

Bible Reading: Genesis 3:8

Lies in the shape of arrows have been aimed at you since before you drew your first breath. The enemy knew you were chosen and formed in the womb by a Father who was completely in love with you.

An overused technique of the enemy is to put the same lie on repeat for all of us. It's a technique that often works if we don't recognize it and call it out because it hits to the innate need we have to be seen that God intentionally placed within us.

Let's expose that lie now:

God's too busy and too far removed to care for what you're going through.

That's what the enemy wants you to believe, and anytime he can reinforce the lie through whispers in your ear, media, others, or events in the news or even in your own personal life, he will use it each and every time.

How could a God who loves the people of Israel, allow the holocaust?
He must not be real.

How could a God who loves people, allow that sweet baby to die?
He must not have heard.

How could a God who loves people, allow that to happen in my life?
He must not care.

The number one lie of the enemy is this:
God is far off, and won't hear you, you are alone, and nobody cares about you.

Sweet sister, everything we have learned about God's hand in the lives of Abraham, Isaac, Jacob, Moses, and our friend at the well, tells us that the heart of God is knit in a love consumed passionate pursuit for you. He's a lover of details and His Presence is so very near. Even now. He's right there with you.

Do you live in that reality? When was the last time you truly sensed His presence?

To look at what life was meant to be before the lie, we have to go back to the beginning, to a garden, lush grass, soft winds, gentle whispers, and purity.

Let's turn to Genesis chapter 1 and 2 and look at what we can learn about the character of God before the fall of man, and the ruling of the prince of the air.

Read Genesis 1:24 and 26 and record what you learn about God:

Did you see the beauty in two little marks on the page? They are quotes. They indicate a sentence spoken.

"Let us make man in our own image".

He was speaking to Himself, the beautiful Trinity, the Father, the Son Jesus, and the Spirit together.

The heart of the Trinity is the essence of community. The indwelling of them together, yet with separate personalities making them distinct. Fully together, fully one, fully functioning together seamlessly, and yet distinct in their responsibilities. The heart of God is a lover of communication, friendship, conversations.

Read Genesis 2:18:

"It's not good for a man to be alone".

So much truth in a sentence with less than 10 words. Have you watched reality tv shows that take a man or women into the wilderness and leaves them alone with minimal supplies for a period of time? They all share a similar progression of decline. They start off strong with great intentions. When hunger sets in they make every attempt at survival the best they can. However when the evenings come and quiet surrounds their camp and there's nobody to talk to things get real. In fact I'd argue to say that's where the real life challenge begins: Loneliness.

Recently, Keith and I watched a documentary on the maximum security facility called Red Onion. The prison is made up mostly of inmates that have attempted escape or caused harm to another individual while in a prison system. As a result they are sent to Red Onion and into isolation. Confined to a small room and left completely alone 23 hours a day, 7 days a week, several of the prisoners confessed that the hardest part, to not losing their mind, was the isolation.

No. It is most certainly *not* good for a man or woman to be alone. Thank you Lord for friendship, for another set of eyes that we can look into, and for the sound of our loved one's voice.

In a world that is scattered with decay and ruled by the prince of isolation, we know that we are most vulnerable when we are alone.

If you want to see the heart of God, look to the polar opposite of the schemes of the enemy. Isolation is the one of his largest weapons. If he can trap you into the lies that you're alone, unloved, and forgotten he can throw a party because he has successfully bound you in lies.

But God.

Two words. There was community in the garden when God spoke with man. Evenings were spent with Adam and Eve walking in the cool of the garden. Abraham spoke to God like a friend, face to face, we can see that God loves relationship. God loves friendship and conversation.

Out of our journey thus far, record what you have learned about the heart and pursuit of Jesus <u>towards the people</u> in Scripture that we have studied?

Out of our journey thus far, record what you have learned about the heart and pursuit of Jesus <u>towards you</u>:

Praise Jesus, the one who waits for us at the well, who watches us as we approach. The One who looks with longing towards us, desires us and has been planning for the day when we will be with him forever. Praise the day when we will sit in His Presence, hear His voice, and bask in His Light.

Last week we identified that Christ Jesus says we will call Him 'My Husband'.

Write below the elements of a healthy marriage:

I'd like to jump in and add a few of my own and hopefully you've written these down too: Courtship, time together, honesty, communication (by both people), truly listening with the heart, not just hearing.

Sweetest one, this is the essence of what your life with Jesus should look like:

Two-way communication, honesty, and dialogue.
Questions and then answers.
Passion.
His anticipation for the next words out of your lips, and your anticipation for the

next words out of His.

If any part of your relationship with Jesus lacks the above, I want you to resolve right now that you are not satisfied with a lack luster marriage to Jesus, but that you crave deeper, Divine Intimacy.

Intimacy always requires two people. If your heart is prompted, stop right now and share those desires for intimacy with Him. Speak to the Spirit and tell Him you desire eyes to see Jesus, ears familiar to the sound of His voice. Ask Jesus to show you Who he truly is so that you can be who you were meant to be: Unveiled, intimately connected and beautiful in his sight.

Let's dig this well a few feet deeper and see what we uncover.

In my 20's I cycled in and out of sin, and pits that were so deep and dark they tasted like death. In all of my wanderings, in all of my self-pursuits, and in all of the times that I believed the enemy, it only ever led to one ending: Loneliness.

When I met my sweet husband Keith, I knew for certain that he was the one God had intended for me. My folks and I would kneel next to the couch and cry out to God for Him to bring the husband that was meant for me. My continuous struggle with purity caused my cries to God to grow louder and louder as I fell from one pit to another. One sweet, sweet day, the faithfulness and love of God showed up with blue eyes, a crooked smile.

A few short months into our married life I realized with a cold hard punch to the gut that my sweet, amazing, and very human husband wasn't the answer to the longings of my heart. Even he didn't have enough in him to fill up my longings. Empty. Dry. Again.

Let's turn back to the only place we know to go now: The well. Look with me at John 4:6.

"Jacob's well was there, and Jesus, worn out from His journey, sat down at the well. It was about six in the evening".

The word used for "well" above, is the Greek word, pēgē.

A word study on the original meaning of this word is as follows:

The idea of gushing plumply. A fount. A source or supply of water, blood, enjoyment. A fountain.

Now let's turn to verses 11 & 12 and read below:

"Sir," said the woman, "You don't even have a bucket, and the well is deep. So where do You get this 'living water'?

The word used for "well" above in this verse is different from what we saw in verse 6. This word is the greek word, phrear.

A word study on the original meaning of this word is as follows:

a *hole* in the ground (dug for obtaining or holding water or other purposes), i.e. a *cistern* or *well*; figurative an *abyss* (as a *prison*) :- well, pit.

With what you've learned above, write below what are the characteristics of the well where Jesus sat:

Note the two different words and their meanings? Write below the meaning of the Now write the characteristics that our friend uses when she speaks back to Jesus:

While our eyes look below us at the well and through the filtered lies we have believed all of our lives, Jesus looks down at that well and sees the truth of the matter.

On our own, our eyes will look into the darkness of that well and focus on a pit. But when we step closer to Jesus, take His hand and see it through His eyes there is water, life, joy, and abundance.

The well that Jesus spoke about, (pēgē) is a subterranean spring that never runs dry. Constantly flowing, never ceasing, always fresh and waiting to be drank. Jesus in the early verses of Genesis formed the springs that run under our feet, but a well had to be dug by man to access it.

Sweet sister, the Spirit is life giving, abundant water that will never run dry. He will leave us and never allow us to thirst, but it took a Man to dig that well for us to get us there: Jesus.

We can dig our holes, but Jesus is the water in our well.

After all a hole without water is only a pit.

As we finish off today, I want you to do an activity that I am going to call critical. It will take some time, but I can't overstate the power behind what you'll do, and the treasures you will unlock. Here's my challenge to you. Find some time in a quiet place. If you have a place in your home, draw away to it. If you have little ones running around, ask your sweet husband, mother or friend if they can watch them for a moment while you hit the nearest coffee shop, but whatever you do, do not skip this portion of the study. It's vital.

Assignment: In the beginning of this study, I asked you to grab a red pen, and anytime you heard the words of the Lord speak to you, to write it in the margin, and underline anything in red. This will be an indicator to you of the moments you heard the Lord speaking to you.

At the end of each week, you would have found a page to recap all of the writing in red, that you should have summarized.

Now, in the back of this book, you will find many pages with lines, all blank and waiting for words. I want you to go through this journey from Week 1, Week 4, and write down everything you wrote or underlined in red.

Tomorrow we are going to dissect His words to you, but I have a sneaking suspicion that after you do this assignment, you're going to meet me back here with a clear picture of what He's saying to you and write it below.

I'll see you tomorrow.

HEARING HIS VOICE & WRITTEN IN RED

Day Three: Leaving Our Jar

"So the woman left her water jar and went away into town…"
John 4:28

PRAY ALOUD AND ASK THE LORD TO OPEN YOUR EYES TO THE TRUTH HE HAS WAITING FOR YOU, AND ASK HIM TO TUNE YOUR EARS TO HEAR HIS VOICE.

Bible Reading: Acts 8

As I write this third day of our last week of studying together, I am currently tucked into an overstuffed chair gazing over the Blue Ridge mountains as the fog rolls between the hills and the sun rises to the east. I can hear my husband softly snoring in the next room and the coffee pot is percolating. These are quiet, special moments in life to sit, ponder, pray, rest in Jesus and have quiet morning conversations with Him. Wilderness always leads me to worship.

This morning after a long week of work and a very long week ahead, it would have been easy to stay in bed, but I could hear a gentle nudging and a soft calling. I had an opportunity for obedience. Obedience to respond to the invitation to enjoy a quiet morning next to Jesus. A year ago the Lord gave me this study and when He did, it left me flat on my face before God. The study came to me with such clarity and beautifully connected.

It's easy to worship with arms outstretched while there is music in the air and the drums beat. In those moments it's also easy to hear promptings and feel a nudging from the Lord. Walking into the busy, demanding world and doing the things the Lord just whispered to you, is another matter entirely.

Sweet friend, we want our lives to be so saturated with the Spirit that the overflow translates into passionate action. Community worship is to be treasured as we gather together to rejoice, but whether it's in the walls of worship or it's during your quiet time, if He asks you to do something, steward that thing to its completion.

We know we are called to greater things, but the Lord entrusts us with talents that He expects we will use for His purpose and His glory. Anything less than the act of 'doing' is disobedience when we receive a Word from the Lord.

Today we pick up our lesson by returning to the well and witnessing the transition from a broken woman, to one so filled with passion, it translates into action. Her experience with Jesus, His truly knowing her and His prophetic word, changed the trajectory of her life in one vulnerable conversation.

We aren't told anything about the man she was living with, except that he wasn't her husband. Nothing else is said about him. We can only assume he didn't see the value in asking her.

When you are in a spiral of sin, without Jesus there's no place to go but down. It would be a safe assumption to make that this man wasn't a gentle, caring, loving partner. In fact, abuse is often bred from control. Our friend likely had few if any possessions, and most of what she had at her finger tips was likely owned by the man she lived with. Oh girls, I can so relate to her. When you're in that type of relationship, making sure you care for his objects isn't just done out of respect and concern, but out of fear.

Although Scripture indicates she brought a water jar, we don't know if it belonged to her or to him. In fact, it likely doesn't matter. Today we return to the moment where she leaves the water jar to run back into town. Leaving such a valuable treasure as a water jar would likely not escape a negative reaction from the man she lived with.

Leaving that water jar meant casting off any thought of that which controlled her.

Women with backgrounds of abuse will be able to relate to this. When you suffer at the hand of someone, you'll do anything in your power not to draw out their anger. My husband calls it "walking on egg shells". I can't think of a more appropriate term for it. Leaving a vessel that was responsible for your life (it held the most important commodity that there was) wouldn't have been wise, let alone elicited a positive response from an abuser.

Leaving her water jar meant leaving her plans and realigning her priorities.

She had come with one purpose (to fetch water for the day), but she was flexible enough to stop, speak with the stranger, engage in dialogue. Her heart was soft enough to respond in vulnerability but she carried grit enough to take action. The mark of change in her couldn't be more distinct. Once a woman who was evading the town as much as possible by gathering in the heat of the day (John 4:6), now we have a woman running towards those same people to tell them about a man who told her everything she had ever done. That's a far cry from being a woman who was wanting to hide her shame.

When Jesus encounters you and you have an experience with Him, you will be changed. You can't see the face of Grace, hear the Voice that causes mountains to shake and tremble, and remain completely the same both inwardly and outwardly.

Whether you've been a follower of Jesus all your life or you are just meeting Him now, if you haven't had a fresh encounter that takes you to your knees, do not finish this lesson without asking for a fresh anointing of the Holy Spirit. He love facilitating fresh encounters with Christ.

When He calls, we must answer. When He speaks, we must listen. None of this comes from a position of 'ought to'. It should all be rooted and growing out of a passionate desire to respond to Him with love pouring out of you towards Him. Our heart posture should be expectant. If He asks anything of us, it should make us want to jump all in, leave the jar and run to do it. That's relationship.

Religion is the requirement of steps. Relationship is the involuntary run to do whatever it is that pleases Him.

Look up Hebrews 12: 1 and write it out at length below:

"Let us lay aside every weight…, and let us run with endurance…".

Girls, it's time to identify our jar.

You may find that in this time of self-analysis you have one large jar, or maybe you have several. Before you begin this time of stepping away and looking honestly at your heart, ask the Holy Spirit to help you have an accurate view of yourself and your situation.

The Spirit may already be prompting you and you know exactly what the label says on your jar. Or you may need to allow yourself to sit in silence and have the Spirit show it to you.

HERE ARE A FEW INDICATORS OF WHAT YOUR JAR MIGHT LOOK LIKE:

A jar can be anything that holds a priority higher than sitting and listing to Jesus.

A jar can be anything or anyone that requests action contrary to what Jesus wants in your life.

A jar can be bondage and reminders of sin.

A jar can be anything that you need to leave behind to go and do what God has put in your heart to do.

Once you've identified what the jar(s) are, I want you to list them in the space below and as you write it, I want you to surrender them to Jesus, and ask the Spirit to cause you to leave them with Him.

Darling friends I'm certain we have never lived in a time where we have more demands, more standards to meet, and more expectations upon us. Today I think we could all use a fresh reminder that the only standard that we have is Jesus.

In last week's study we looked at Jesus's reaction when the Father asked Him to go. Look back at your notes and highlights from Week 4, Day 1. **Write below anything that speaks to you about Jesus's action:**

Ladies, we are more than ambassadors of Christ. We are His bride. As His bride, our desires, plans, and goals should be in alignment with His priorities. If that's the case, we need to identify where our Samaria is. If Jesus said "I must needs go", He was saying that the Father was working in Samaria and He needed to join Him there to complete the work.

Turn with me to Acts chapter 8, verses 4 - 8. Write below what takes place in bullet point form:

Now look with me at verse 14, and prior to reading it, I want you to specifically ask the Spirit of God to fall on you and equip you to read this with fresh eyes. Be sensitive to what He shows you. **Write your observations below:**

There wouldn't have been a large expanse of time between John chapter 4 and Acts chapter 8. Jesus was in the middle to end of his ministry. The death and resurrection would have already occurred and 40 days later Jesus would ascend into heaven. Shortly after that Pentecost would happen and that would mark the moment when the people who were entrusted with the message of Christ would start spreading throughout the earth. This is where and why we find Philip in Samaria. We have every reason to believe that he would have been one of the disciples with Jesus when he met the woman at the well.

Sweetest one, just like Philip and the other disciples, when we go to our places we call Samaria, we might just find the harvest is ripe because Jesus has already been there.

Let's spend some time this morning identifying the Samaria that the Spirit is putting into our heart.

To help us identify where or what that might be, here are a few indicators of what your Samaria might look like:

A place where nobody else wants to go.

A place where the forgotten reside.

A place that may have shame associated with it.

A place where people tell you not to go.

A place of disgrace.

A place of your past.

We have had a lot of time this morning asking the Spirit to speak to us and reveal to us the personal application He wants us to apply with the concepts and truth we have learned. As we close our study time together today, let's ask the Spirit to reveal to you where your Samaria might be, I want you to write it below, and include what He is asking you to do. It could be there's a rock of unforgiveness that needs to be overturned. Whatever it may be, I'm confident the Holy Spirit will walk with you hand in hand and reveal it to you. I'll see you tomorrow sweet one.

HEARING HIS VOICE & WRITTEN IN RED

Day Four: Our Ministry

"I planted the seed, Apollos watered it, but God made it grow. So neither he who plants nor he who waters is anything, but only God, who makes things grow. The man who plants and the man who waters have one purpose, and each will be rewarded according to his own labor"

I Corinthians 3:6-8

PRAY ALOUD AND ASK THE LORD TO OPEN YOUR EYES TO THE TRUTH HE HAS WAITING FOR YOU, AND ASK HIM TO TUNE YOUR EARS TO HEAR HIS VOICE.

Bible Reading: John 4: 34 - 42

In day 2 of our study this week we went back and pulled out all the places in red where we felt the Lord had been speaking to us. We wrote it in the back of our book and before we dive into our lesson for today, I want us to find our plot of land where the Lord is calling us individually.

Below you are going to go to the back of your book and summarize the notes you made of things written in red. Before you begin I want you to be sure you check your posture. Begin on your knees (literally) before the Most High God, and ask Him to clean out your clutter, give you a new heart, and eyes to see where He is working. Posture before our King is everything. Go ahead and start listing out the theme or words He said to you:

By now you should have a clear indication of where you feel the Lord is moving you and things He alone is putting on your heart.

We are *all* called to something. As a mother, your calling to raise children is equally as important as the woman who is the President of a large organization. If your platform is an audience of a few kids, that calling is equally as important as it is on a stage. I think it would do us all a lot of good if we stopped demanding the type of seed we are wanting to sow and we come humbly to the Farmer, hands outstretched, and receive what He knows He needs planted.

Today we are going to dive into what we call the 'Principle Of The Harvest'. I wish we could meet together on a farm. There's something beautiful about the image in my head of bread baking in the oven, rocking chairs with cold glasses of sweet tea on the porch and a view of corn fields as far as the eye can see waving in the wind. All of it is in praise to its Creator. There is a gentle call from the cows in a nearby field, and the kids run wild next to the dogs, while the chickens scratch at the earth.

In all this farm life beauty let's not forget that hands labored over the kneading of that baking bread. Another pair of hands reached into a bag of seed and spent days planting each one in the field. A craftsman cut the pieces of wood to create that rocking chair, and someone of course has to tend to and feed the cows.

Let's not miss looking at the work of stewarding the seeds. We are all given seeds, the question is do we have the passion and the grit for what it takes to get it in the ground.

Together let's read John 4:34 - 42 and fill in the blanks:

"Do you not say, 'there are yet _____, then comes the harvest'? Look, I tell you, _____, and see that the fields are white for _____. Already the one who reaps is receiving wages and gathering fruit for _____, so that the _____ and _____ may rejoice together. For here the saying holds true, '_____.' I sent you to reap that for which you did not labor. _____ have labored, and _____ have eternal into their labor.'

Don't put off what you can do today for tomorrow.

      The Farmer who has sowed the seed in the spring, watered throughout the season, fertilized as necessary, is the one who at the end of the day can dust the dirt from his britches, sit on that rocking chair to take in the beauty with a deep breath, can do so with a sigh of satisfaction because He knows the harvest is ready.

Let's look at 1 Corinthians 3:6-8 and write below who owns which task:

      Sweet one, I wonder how many of us feel called to do big things for Jesus, but we aren't passionate or committed to being faithful with the small things He asks us to do. In the realm of the kingdom of heaven, a Spirit timed hand-written encouragement note to someone who is deeply in need is just as vital and important as a message delivered to thousands.

      When my daughter turned 16 and got her license, she immediately went to work. We didn't give her a car or throw money into her account. Instead she began with little and slowly grew it day by day. She did so well that it was our delight to help her financially when she go tto college because she had been found faithful with the little things while in High School.

The same is true of our relationship with Jesus as our Father. Stewarding the small seeds today will always be rewarded with a rich harvest of His favor.

Read Ephesians 5:16 and write it out below:

How do you feel this verse applies to what God is saying to your heart right now?

DON'T FALL INTO THE TRAP BELIEVING YOU HAVE TO MAKE THINGS HAPPEN:

Here's the long and short of it. If God has put it on your heart, He will do the work of opening the doors to get you to that place He is working. Let God be God.

I've found in my life that anytime I have to force a door open, climb out through a window, or jump over hurdles to reach the door, I'm likely stepping out of God's plan. The door may be intended for me to walk through, but He hasn't led me to the time/place of being ready to put my hand on the doorknob.

A promise from God may include a vision for something He's put on your heart, but there are many items He needs to move around in your life before He can get you to the threshold.

SOME DAYS YOU'LL SOW AND SOME DAYS YOU'LL REAP.

Sowers and reapers are often different people. In the example of John chapter 4 and Acts 8, Jesus had sowed the seeds in one woman's life, who then planted more seeds in the town. Jesus was the One who brought the harvest by spending days with them and teaching them.

When we sow, we sow unto the Lord. We do this by planting the seeds He has given us. We go to the field he assigned to us. Obedience is the essence of worship. We can only reap in the places Christ has visited and where He assigns us.

SOWING SEEDS IN WIDE OPEN SPACES

Nobody plants a seed and the next day sees the corn field ripe with corn. That's not the principle of the harvest. The principle of the harvest is working by faith with daily confidence that the harvest will come. Some days those fields will be lonely while you work alone in the mundane. Blog posts you've written will seem like you're writing to a wall and that meal you take to a neighbor may seem relatively insignificant, but those moments of doing the assigned work, is all that God asks. Just because you can't see the audience who witnesses the obedience, doesn't mean there isn't one there.

Let's look at Ephesians 3: 7- 12

One commentary summarizes this verse and its implications perfectly when he says this:

"The Church becomes a mirror through which the bright ones of heaven see the glory of

God. And in order to show them this glory, God committed the gospel to Paul" (Beet, 1877-90)

Sweet sister, let that sink in. The bright ones of heaven (angels) stand and watch to see what we are doing so they can observe the glory of God. If you need a larger audience than that, I am going to strongly recommend counseling.

STEWARD THE SINGLE SEEDS AND YOU'LL BE ENTRUSTED WITH HARVESTS.

Girls, before we close today let's look at Luke 12: 42 - 48.

> *"And the Lord answered, "Who then is the faithful and wise manager, whom the master puts in charge of his servants to give them their portion at the proper time?*
>
> *Blessed is that servant whom his master finds doing so when he returns.*
>
> *Truly I tell you, he will put him in charge of all his possessions.*
>
> *But suppose that servant says in his heart, 'My master will be a long time in coming,' and he begins to beat the male and female servants, and to eat and drink and get drunk.*
>
> *The master of that servant will come on a day when he does not expect him, and at an hour of which he is unaware. Then He will cut him to pieces and assign him a place with the unbelievers.*
>
> *That servant who knows his master's will but does not get ready or follow his instructions will be beaten with many blows.*
>
> *But the one who unknowingly does things worthy of punishment will be beaten with few blows.* **From everyone who has been given much, much will be required; and from him who has been entrusted with much, even more will be demanded."**

Out of everyone Jesus could have chosen to use to bring an entire city to Him, He chose one broken woman with a shameful past, an outcast, who in her brokenness could clearly see Jesus for who He is: The Savior and Prince she had been needing. It was the words from His lips, the tender love in His eyes that transformed this woman radically in a single conversation. A radical change in our lives is a direct result of intimacy with Christ. When it happens we have no choice but to share it. Much in the same way a lovesick teenager can't stop talking about her crush, let's have that same obsession with our Prince at the well. Let's do everything we can to please Him in our obedience to what He is asking us to do.

HEARING HIS VOICE & WRITTEN IN RED

Day Five: Jesus: Our Prince, Our First And Our Last

"Who has measured the waters in the hollow of his hand and marked off the heavens with a span, enclosed the dust of the earth in a measure and weighted the mountains in scales and the hills in a balance? Who has measured the Spirit of the Lord…"

Isaiah 40: 12 - 13

PRAY ALOUD AND ASK THE LORD TO OPEN YOUR EYES TO THE TRUTH HE HAS WAITING FOR YOU, AND ASK HIM TO TUNE YOUR EARS TO HEAR HIS VOICE.

Bible Reading: John 4:39 - 42

It jumped off the page and hit me square in the eyes. The Word of God is alive, active, and sharper than a two edged sword. A story I had read and heard taught thousands of times before, hit me like a sucker punch in the gut and brought me to my knees. Tearfully I went to my sweet parents and shared with them the 'Word' I had received. My dad looked me in the eyes and said "that will preach". That was the day this Bible Study was birthed.

Somewhere along the way I had placed those who write Bible studies on a platform thinking they had it all together and yet here as I sit writing the very last day to this Bible Study, I certainly confess I don't have it all together. Far from it.

"Lord, how do I come to this study with these fresh wounds that I have broken open" was my anthem this morning.

He then whispered these words to me: "That's the essence of this study. It all begins, and ends with me. You must faithfully come back to the well to be refilled and refreshed".

The one thing I know is true is that Jesus is everything and He alone will fill the deepest desires and longings of our heart. No relationship, no calling, no platform, no job, no child can ever fill the holes that were created for Him to fill. And so as we begin this last day and prepare to part ways (at least for now), let's remember that we don't leave our well for long. Our well is a sacred place to us where we will come back weary from the world and as we turn the corner, we will see Him seated next to it, waiting with that perfect smile. And in the distance we'll hear His voice calling our name saying "come".

I hope you'll recall with me the story of Hagar that we studied in week 2. If you'll remember, God called out Hagar by name. Being called by name is everything. It's part of being known. As I wrote this study, I stumbled over how to refer to the woman at the well in John 4. You'll notice I called her "our friend at the well". This was 100% intentional. We can't cast stones to someone that isn't far removed from where we sit. Replace 5 husbands, with 5 lies, 5 moments of gluttony, 5 times we cussed, 5 times we coveted our neighbor, 5 times we judged another. We aren't that different from her, and so as we've travelled this journey with her, we are calling her our friend.

The lack of her name being mentioned allows us to enter into Scripture, and put our name where hers is missing. Broken women are attracted to Jesus, and Jesus is without a doubt attracted to broken women.

Today I want you to turn with me to our reading for today: John 4:39 - 42. Read with me below:

> *"Many of the Samaritans from that town believed in Jesus because of the woman's testimony, 'He told me everything I ever did.' So when the Samaritans came to Him, they asked Him to stay with them, and He stayed two days. And many more believed because of His message. They said to the woman, 'We now believe not only because of your words; we have heard for ourselves, and we know that this man truly is the Savior of the world.'"*

An entire town believed because of the testimony of a broken woman. What's fascinating is that they then returned to her and confirmed their belief to someone who was once cast aside. There's validation in the transformation here.

In the two days Jesus spent teaching, laughter, meals shared, homes visited, and hearts known, gaps were closed, barriers were broken. No longer was there an environment in this town with disputes over territory, race, religion or creed. Jesus, the One who holds all things together was there for one purpose and one purpose only; to rescue.

Verse 42 ends with "we know that this man really is the Savior of the world". The word for "world" is the Greek transliteration, kosmos. This word appears 185 times in the New Testament and John uses it 105 of those times in his writing. However, this phrase, "Savior of the world" appears only here and in 1 John 4:14.

Write 1 John 4:14 in the blank space below:

One commentator said it best this way:

"The expression "Savior of the world" is particularly Johannine. It coordinates magnificently with the baptizer's initial confession of Jesus as the paschal "Lamb of God, who takes away the sin of the world" (John 1:29). John saw Jesus as the answer to the world's need. The people of the world were the focus of God's love in Jesus (3:16). The outcasts of Samaria here articulated the purpose of God because Jesus was their expected *Taheb,* the Savior of the world. Their confession stands as a vivid contrast to the disgust of the Pharisees and the story of the entry into Jerusalem just prior to Passover when in exasperation they finally complained, "The whole world has gone after Him!" (Gangel, Holman New Testament Commentary - John, 2000)

Read Matthew 18: 12 and write your thoughts below and the Truth He speaks to you:

That same story is also record in Luke 15:3-7, but includes this: "And when he has found it, he lays it on his shoulders, rejoicing" (verse 5).

You are His lamb. You will always be His lamb. Some days you'll stray from the Shepherd, and other days you'll be tucked right near His side. Other days you may become wounded from outside sources, unexpected hollows or elements and when you do, you have One who will see you, tenderly pick you up, lay you on his shoulders and bring you home to heal you.

Deep truth comes from a Prince who chooses to leave His Palace to come to the dirt, the poor, the broken, the disgusting, the diseased, the desperate individual: The nameless lamb at the well.

Where religion stops and passionate relationship with our Prince begins is where we realize that He is still waiting at that well, with His hand outstretched, waiting to hear us, heal us, and know us.

As we close this study, allow me to pray this prayer over you:

To the the Prince who waits for us at the well,

We were created with an innate desire to be the damsel who knows she needs saving, and with a passionate desire for a Prince. Arriving at a well, tattered, torn, broken, and used was never part of our childhood dreams and yet here we stand: Dirty and desperate.

Husband of our hearts, may the one who reads this no longer be satisfied with religion, ritual, schedules. vMay the one holding this study see you in a new light and through personal experience arrive at a deeper longing for Your face, Your touch, Your personality to shine through her. Mostly Jesus, give her ears to hear Your whisper.

My prayer for her is that You will wake within her the longings you planted. Her heart is for you (Song of Solomon 8:4). Jesus let her desire be to recognize the sound of Your voice, the tone of your Words and that it would be as familiar as her closest friend.

At times when her well is dried up, stir these Words of Yours in her heart and allure her back to the well where You are waiting for her. Speak tenderly to her (Hosea 2:14).

You are the source of our life, our happiness, our joy, our peace. You are our Prince.

Jesus thank you for all these moments where you have tenderly met us at the well these last weeks. Thank you for revealing your purpose for us and your passionate desire for our hearts. May the close of this study be the gateway to our passionate relationship with You.

HEARING HIS VOICE & WRITTEN IN RED

WEEKLY RECAP

About The Author

Tiffany and her husband Keith reside in Charleston, South Carolina and are professional nature photographers. They own and operate Charleston Photography Tours, The Photography Workshop Company and their online mentorship program, Sharpen Your Shutter.

Her primary passion is ministry and sharing the intimacy that can be had between a longing heart and a loving Savior. She has a ministry group on Facebook called A Quest For Light, and a blog under the same name.

When she's not traveling photographing the beauty of God's creativity, she's at home with her three dogs. Keith & Tiffany have two adult children who are one of her greatest blessings.

You can find more about Tiffany on her blog at www.aquestforlight.com

For her photography you can follow her here: www.tiffanybriley.com

Photography Workshop Company
www.photographyworkshopcompany.com

Charleston Photography Tour
www.charlestonphotographytours.com

Sharpen Your Shutter
www.sharpenyourshutter.com

www.ingramcontent.com/pod-product-compliance
Lightning Source LLC
Chambersburg PA
CBHW080603170426
43196CB00017B/2886